EASY GUITAR WITH NOTES & TAB

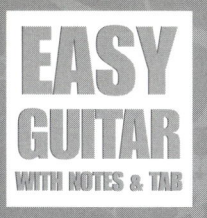

The Songs of Sarah McLachlan

2 *Strum and Pick Patterns*
8 *Adia*
12 *Angel*
3 *Building a Mystery*
16 *Circle*
24 *Do What You Have to Do*
26 *Drawn to the Rhythm*
19 *Elsewhere*
30 *Good Enough*
34 *Hold On*
37 *I Love You*
40 *Ice*
42 *Ice Cream*
44 *Mary*
47 *Plenty*
54 *Possession*
50 *Sweet Surrender*
57 *Wait*
60 *Witness*

Photography by Kharen Hill
Design by Crystal Heald for Artwerks
Special thanks to David Sinclair

ISBN 0-634-00498-0

HAL•LEONARD® CORPORATION
7777 W. BLUEMOUND RD. P.O. BOX 13819 MILWAUKEE, WI 53213

For all works contained herein:
Unauthorized copying, arranging, adapting, recording or public performance is an infringement of copyright.
Infringers are liable under the law.

Visit Hal Leonard Online at
www.halleonard.com

STRUM AND PICK PATTERNS

This chart contains the suggested strum and pick patterns that are referred to by number at the beginning of each song in this book. The symbols ⊓ and ⋁ in the strum patterns refer to down and up strokes, respectively. The letters in the pick patterns indicate which right-hand fingers plays which strings.

p = thumb
i = index finger
m = middle finger
a = ring finger

For example; Pick Pattern 2
is played: thumb - index - middle - ring

Strum Patterns

Pick Patterns

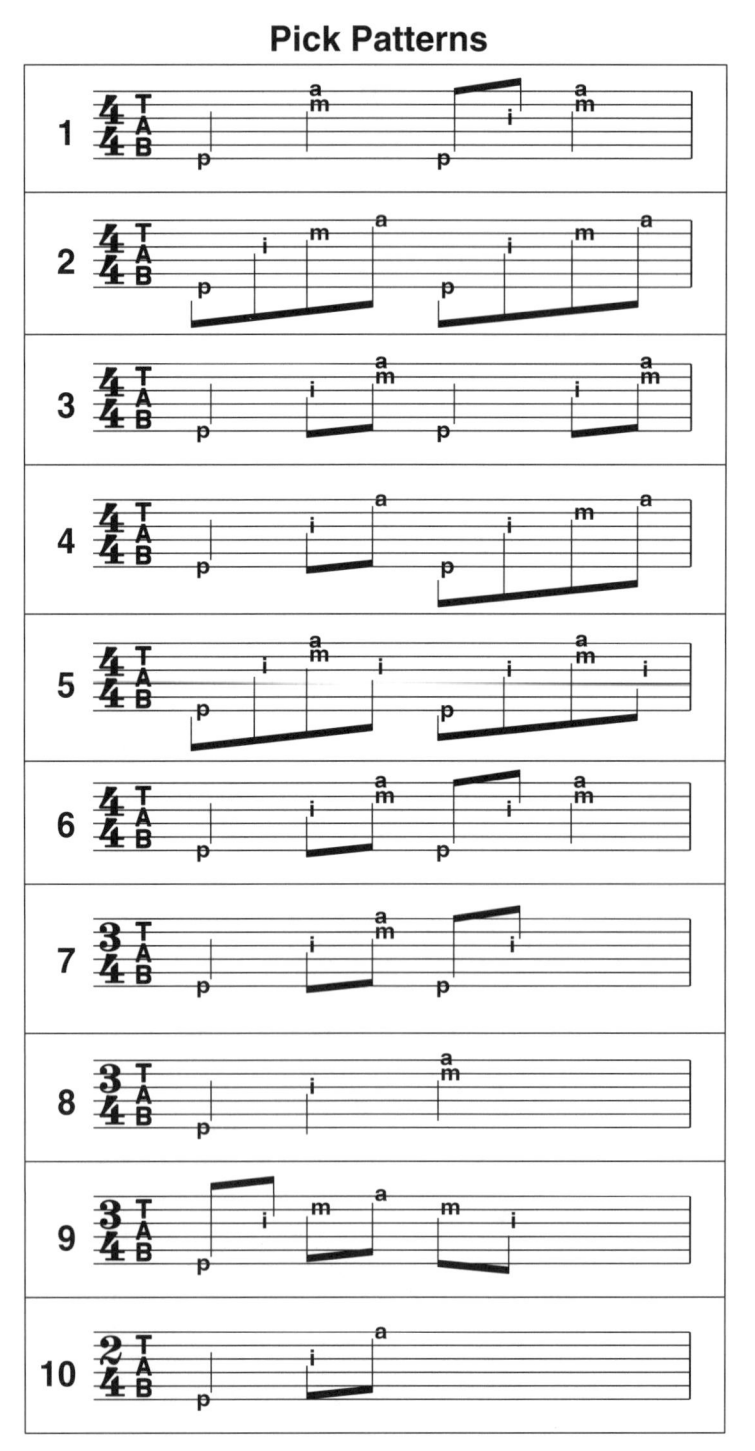

You can use the 3/4 Strum or Pick Patterns in songs written in compound meter (6/8, 9/8, 12/8, etc.). For example, you can accompany a song in 6/8 by playing the 3/4 pattern twice in each measure. The 4/4 Strum and Pick Patterns can be used for songs written in cut time (¢) by doubling the note time values in the patterns. Each pattern would therefore last two measures in cut time.

Building a Mystery

Words and Music by Sarah McLachlan and Pierre Marchand

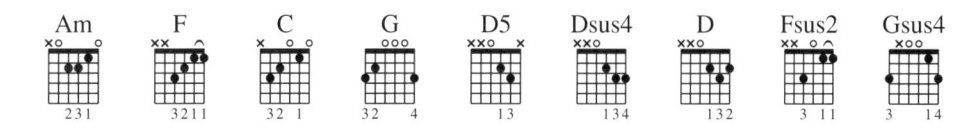

* Strum Pattern: 1, 3
* Pick Pattern: 3, 4

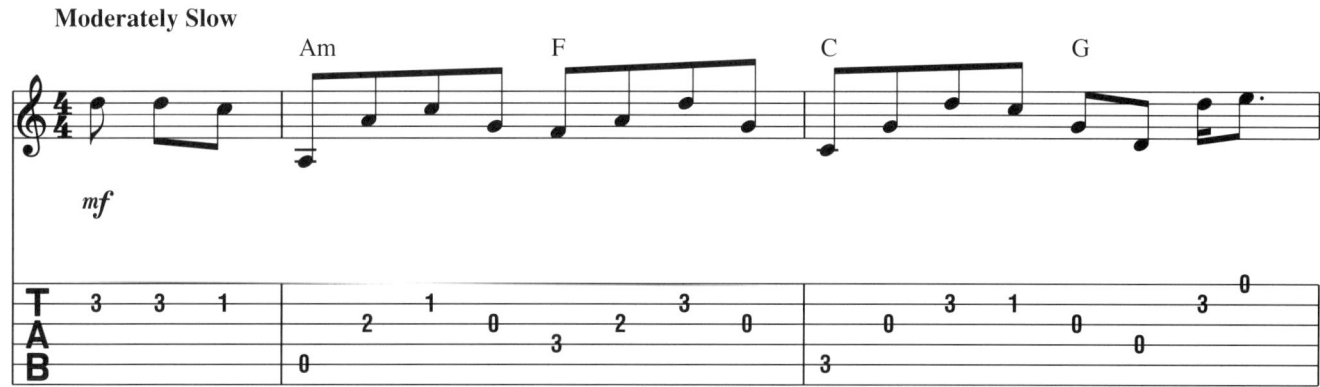

Intro
Moderately Slow

* use pattern 10 for 2/4 meas.

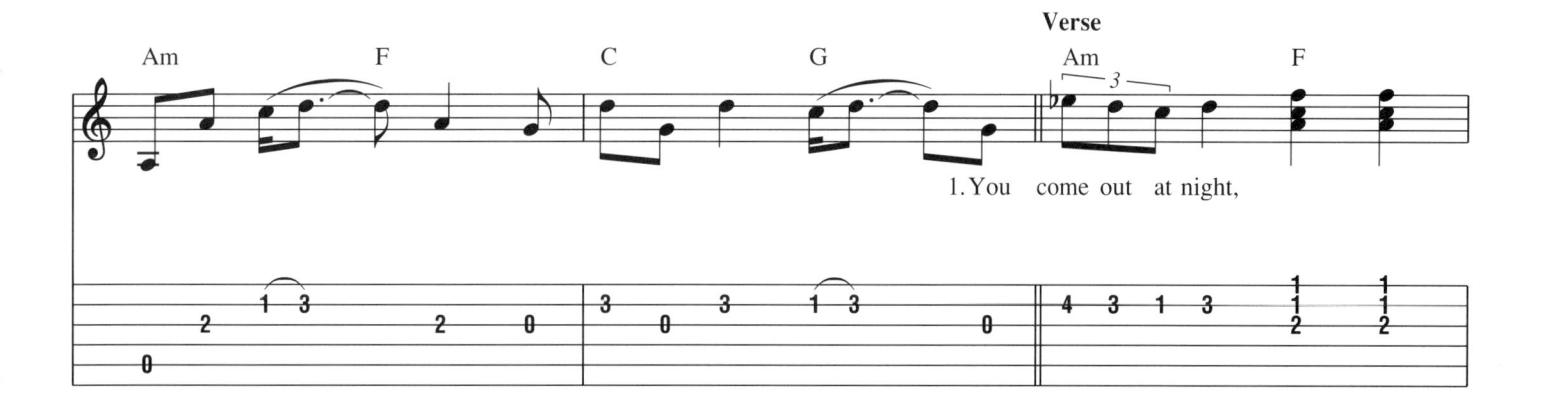

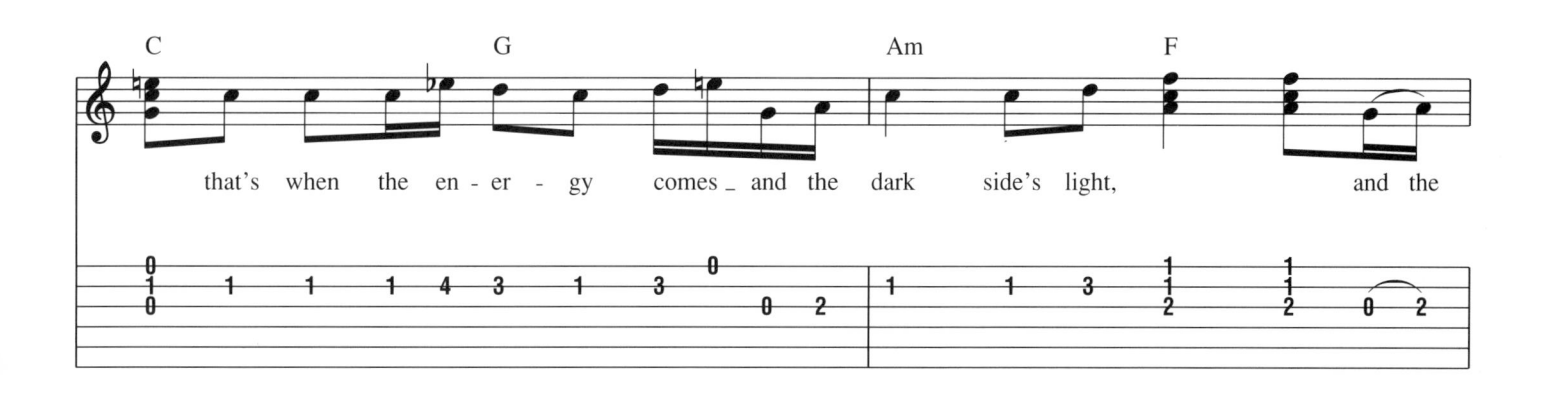

Verse

1. You come out at night, that's when the en-er-gy comes_ and the dark side's light, and the

Copyright © 1997 Sony/ATV Songs LLC, Tyde Music and Pierre J. Marchand
All Rights on behalf of Sony/ATV Songs LLC and Tyde Music Administered by Sony/ATV Music Publishing,
8 Music Square West, Nashville, TN 37203
International Copyright Secured   All Rights Reserved

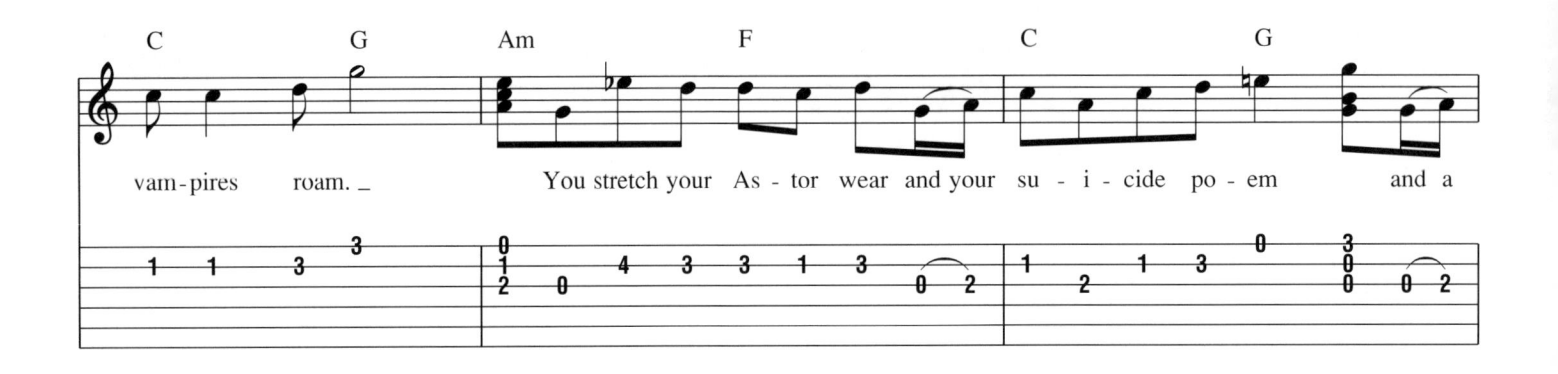

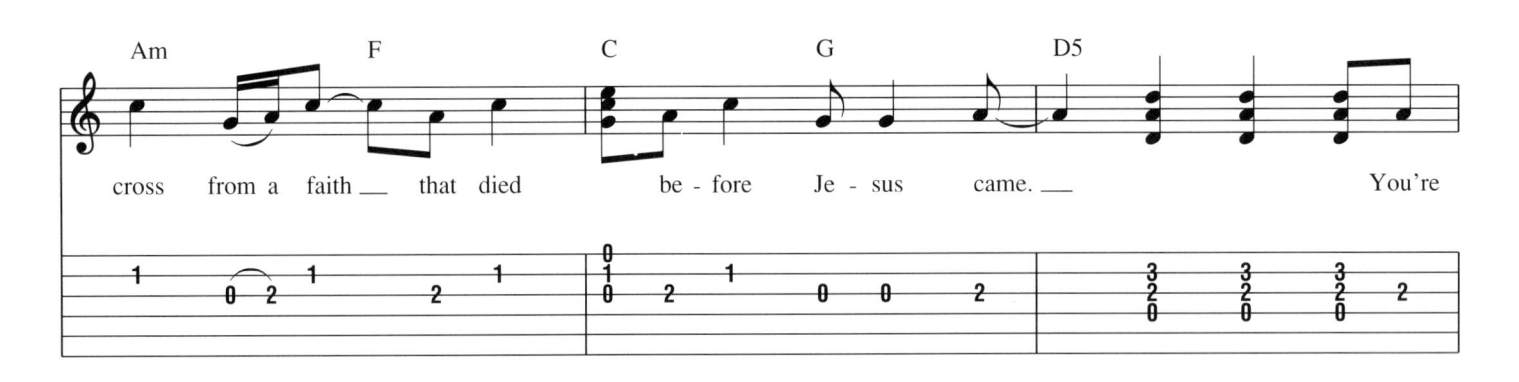

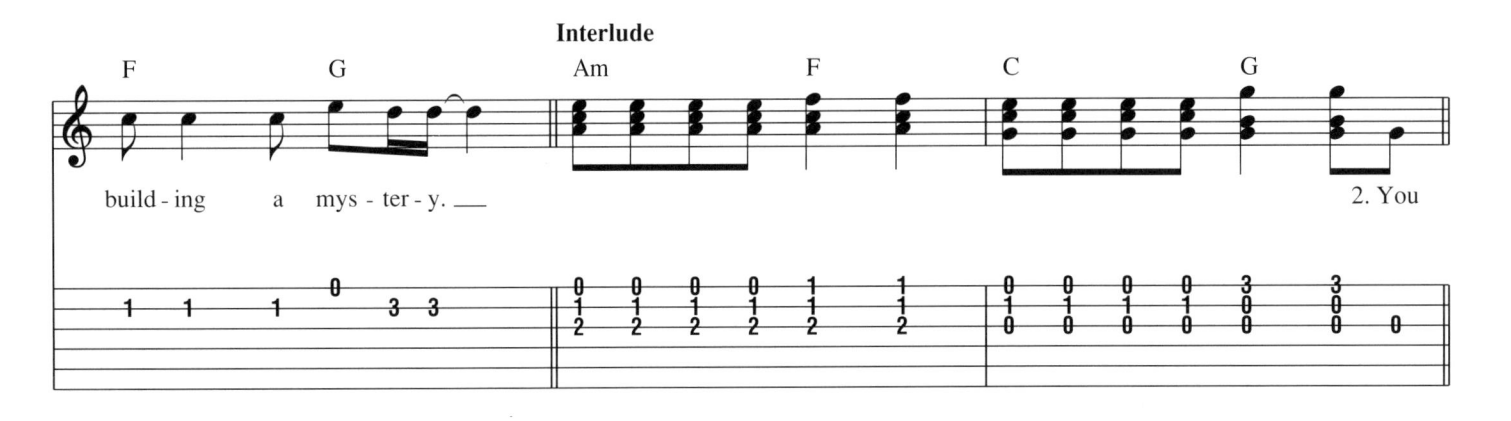

vam-pires roam. You stretch your As-tor wear and your su-i-cide po-em and a cross from a faith that died be-fore Je-sus came. You're building a mys-ter-y.

2. You live in a church where you sleep with voo-doo dolls, and you

3. *See Additional Lyrics*

won't give up the search for the ghost in the halls.

Am F C G
You wear san - dals in the snow and a smile I won't wash a - way.
Am C G
Can you look out the win - dow with-out your shad - ow get - ting in the way?
Dsus4 D Fsus2 Dsus4 D
You're so beau-ti - ful with an edge and charm - ing. You're so care - ful when
Chorus
Fsus2 G Am F C G
I'm in your arms. 'Cause your work - ing, build - ing a mys - ter - y,
Am F C G Am F
hold - ing on and hold - ing it in. Yeah, you're work - ing

C G Am F C G
build - ing a mys - ter - y, and choos - ing so care - ful - ly.
1.
2.
Guitar Solo
F G Fsus2
3. You woke up
D5 F Gsus4 F Gsus4 F
Outro-Chorus
D5 Fsus2 G Am F
Oo, you're work - ing build - ing a mys - ter - y, hold - ing on
C G Am F C G
and hold - ing it in. Yeah, you're work - ing build - ing a mys - ter - y,

Additional Lyrics

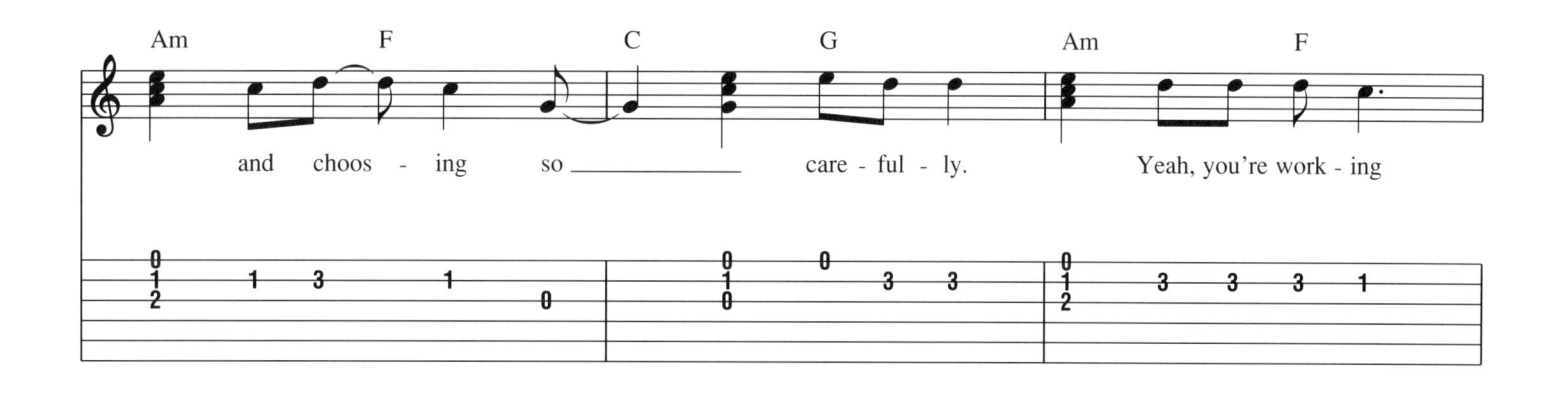

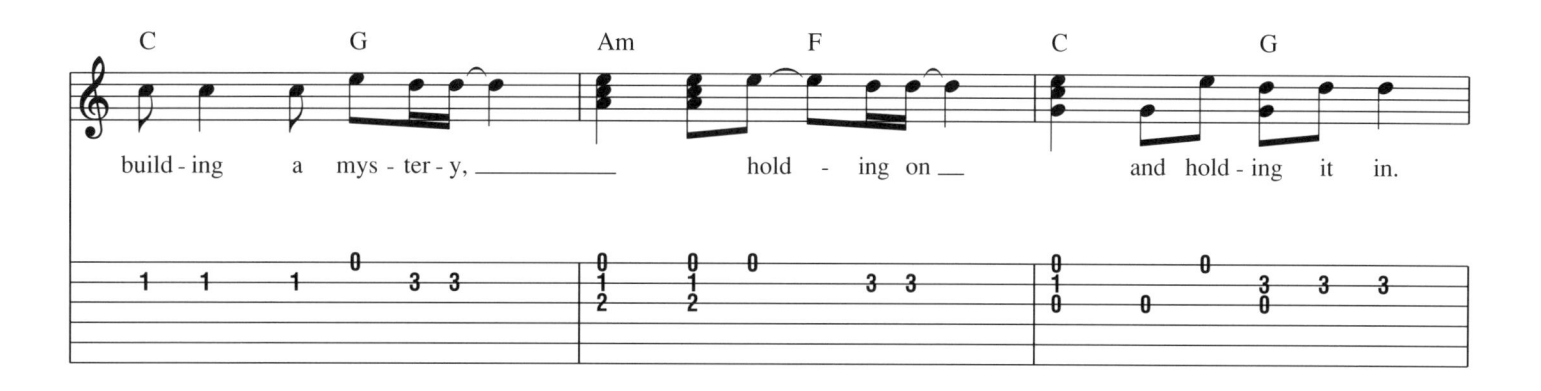

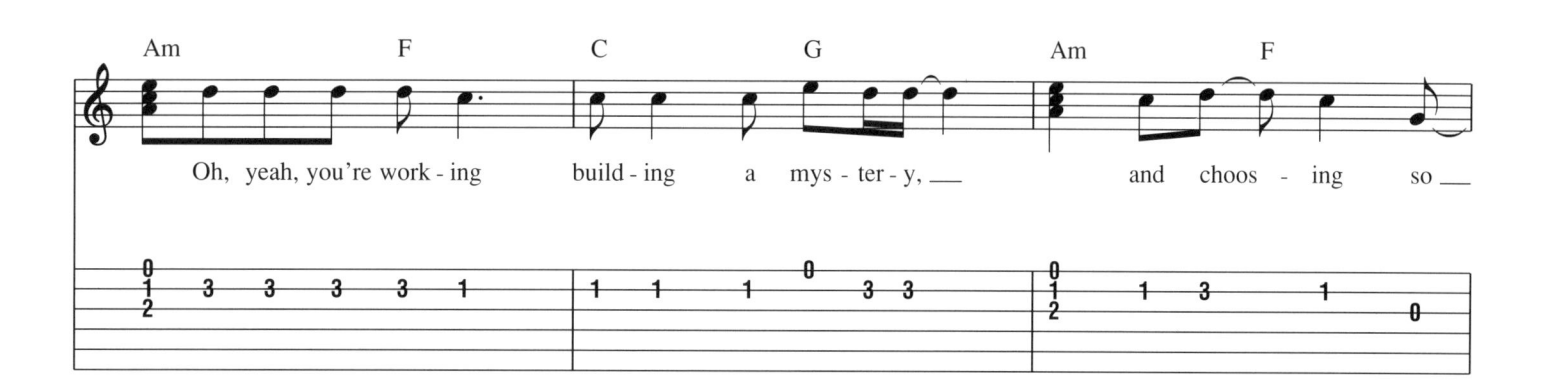

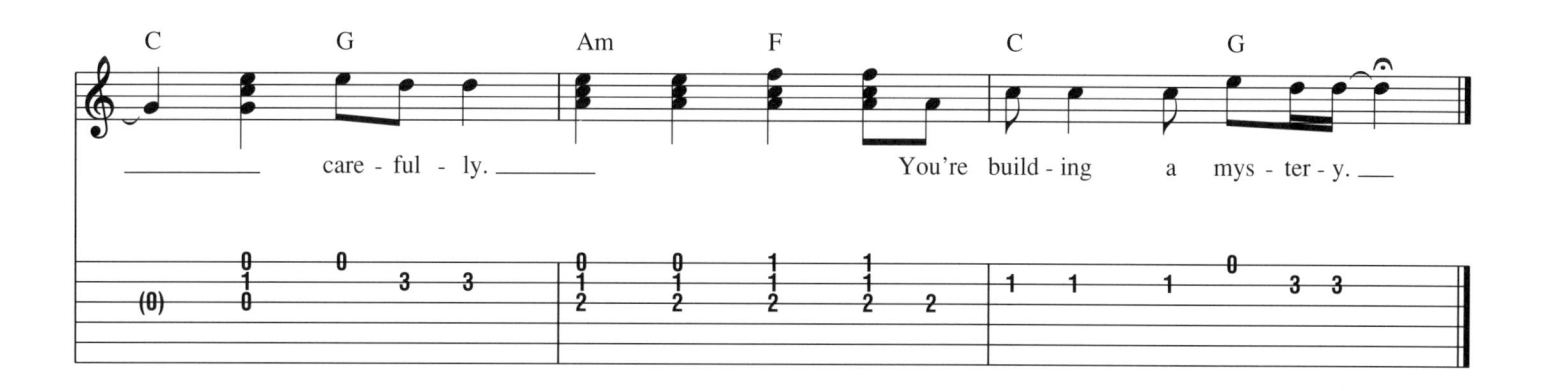

3. You woke up screaming aloud
   A prayer from your secret god to
   Feed off of fears and hold back your tears, oh.
   You give us a tantrum and a know-it-all grin
   Just when you need one, when the evenin' stayed.
   You're a beautiful, a beautiful fucked up man.
   You set it up, you're razor wire sharp.

Adia

Words and Music by Sarah McLachlan and Pierre Marchand

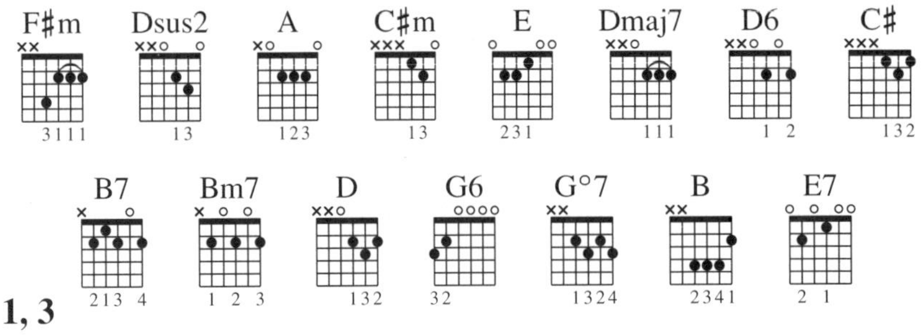

Strum Pattern: 1, 3
Pick Pattern: 2, 4

me. Try-ing to find a way to car-ry on. I search my-self and ev-'ry-one to see where we went wrong. There's no one left to fin-ger. There's no one here to blame. There's no one left to talk to, hon-ey, and there ain't no one to buy our in-no-cence 'cause we are born

Chorus

in - no - cent. Be-lieve me,

D
Bm7
E
C♯m
A - di - a, we are still in - no - cent.
G°7
Bm7
It's eas - y, we all fal - ter. And does it mat -
1.
C♯
2.
C♯
N.C.
- ter? - ter?
Interlude
B7
A
E
F♯m
B
E
E7
'Cause we are born
Chorus
A
G°7
D
in - no - cent. Be - lieve me, A - di - a,

Additional Lyrics

3. Adia, I thought that we could make it.
   I know I can't change the way you feel.
   I leave you with your misery
   A friend who won't betray.
   Pull you from your tower.
   I take away your pain.
   I show you all the beauty you possess
   If you'd only let yourself believe that…

Angel

Words and Music by Sarah McLachlan

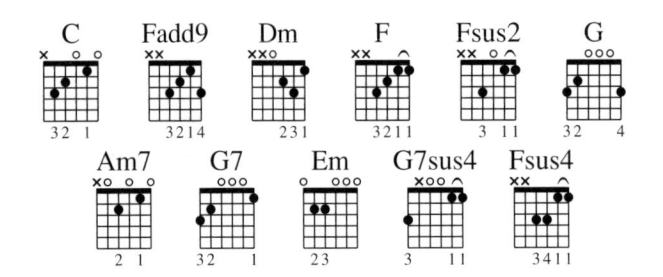

Chords: C, Fadd9, Dm, F, Fsus2, G, Am7, G7, Em, G7sus4, Fsus4

Strum Pattern: 8, 9
Pick Pattern: 7, 8

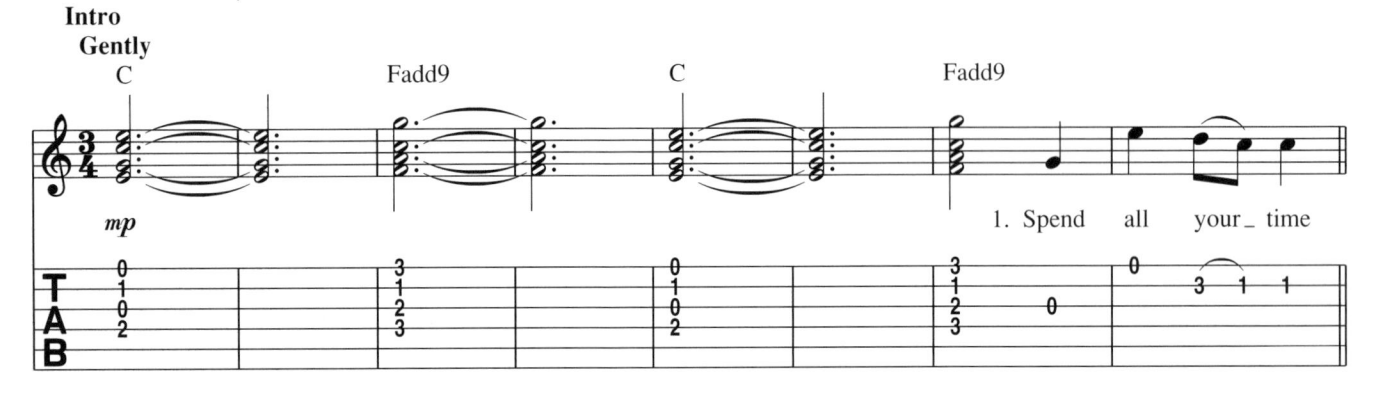

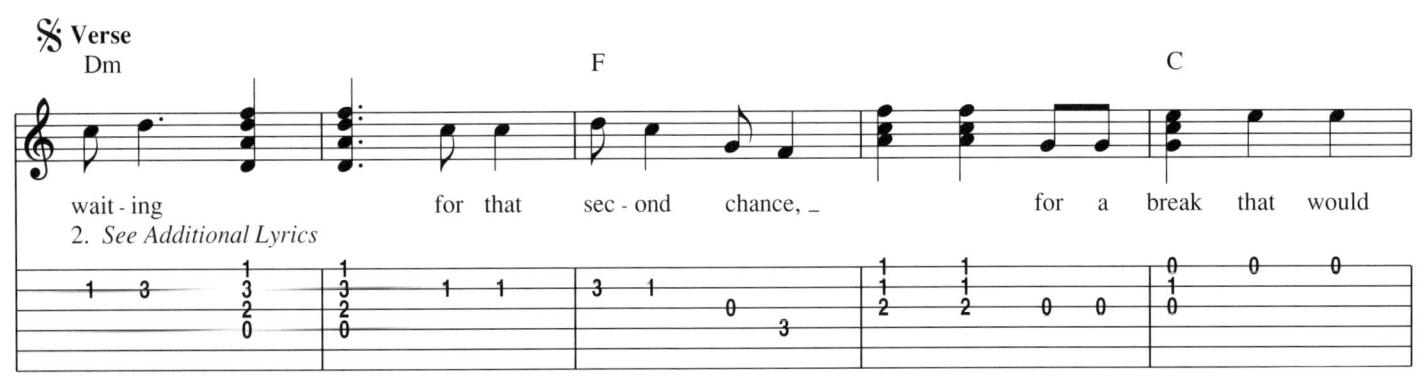

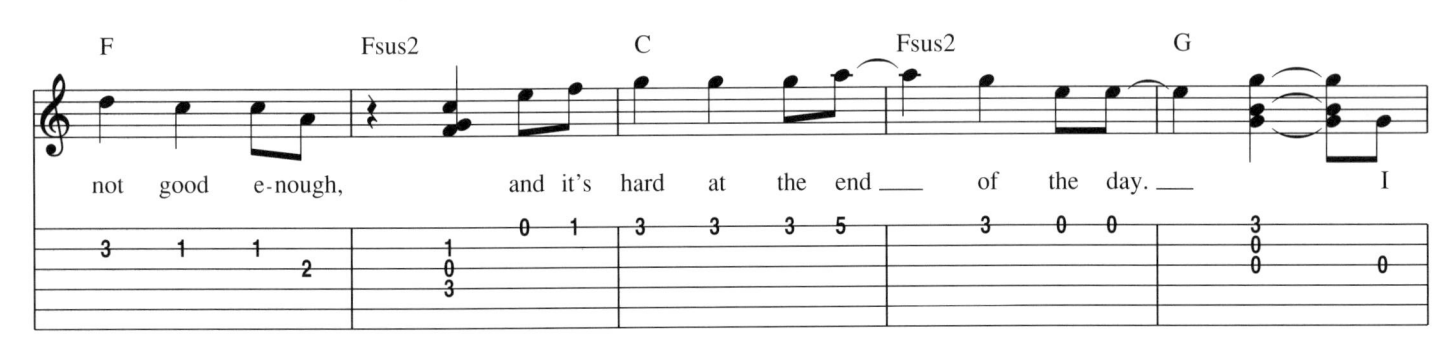

Intro
Gently

mp

1. Spend all your time

Verse

Dm — wait-ing
2. *See Additional Lyrics*

F — for that sec-ond chance,

C — for a break that would

Fsus2 — make it o-kay.

G — There's al-ways some rea-son

Dm — to feel

F — not good e-nough,

Fsus2 C — and it's hard at the end

Fsus2 G — of the day. I

Copyright © 1997 Sony/ATV Songs LLC and Tyde Music
All Rights Administered by Sony/ATV Music Publishing, 8 Music Square West, Nashville, TN 37203
International Copyright Secured   All Rights Reserved

12

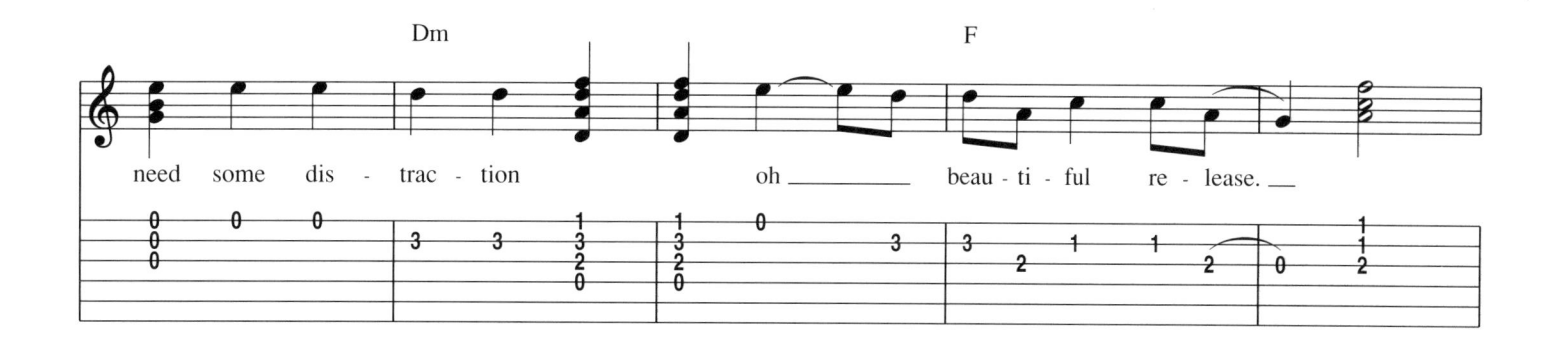

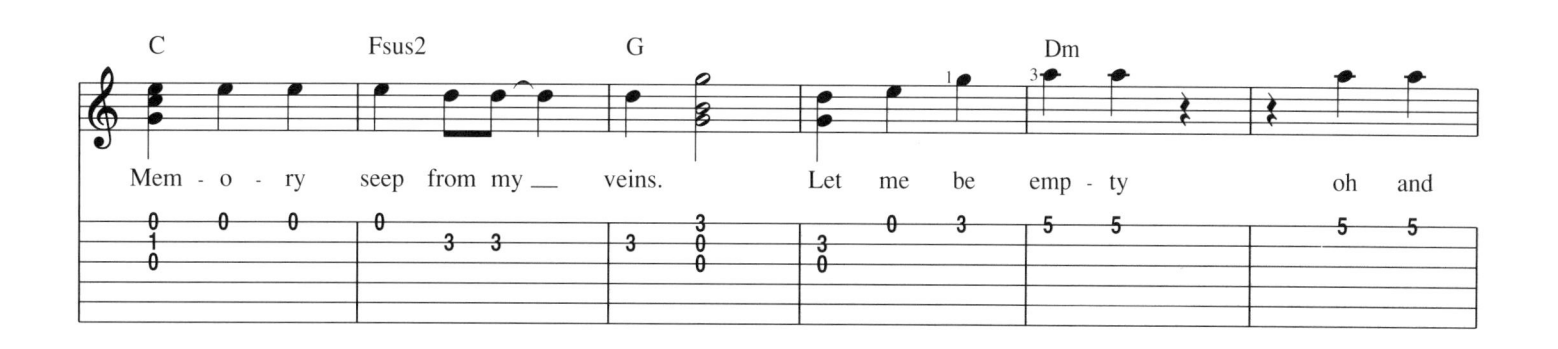

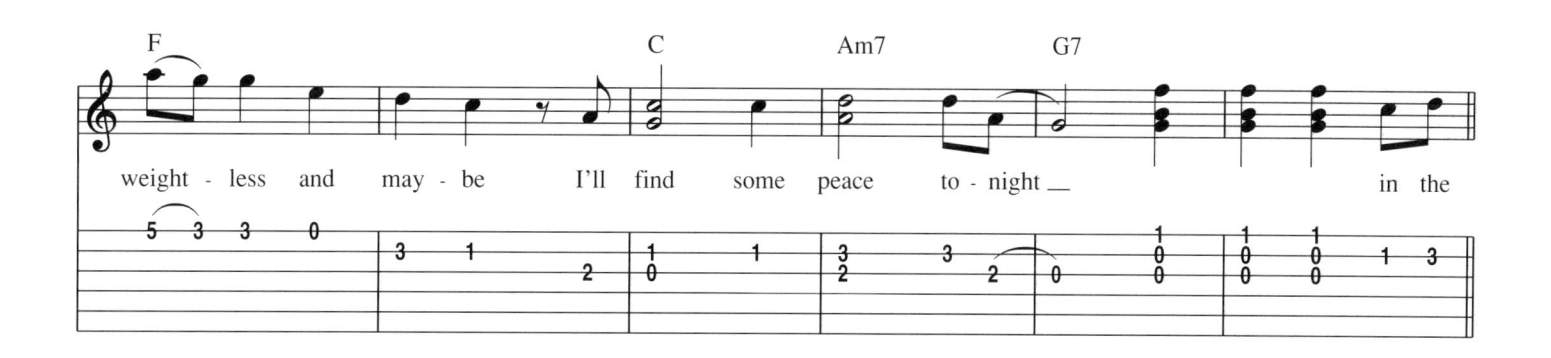

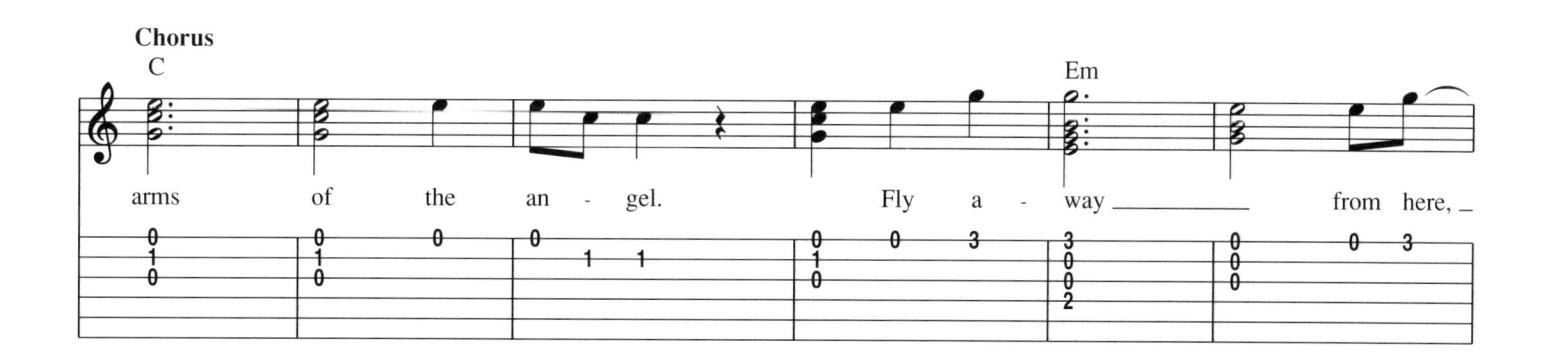

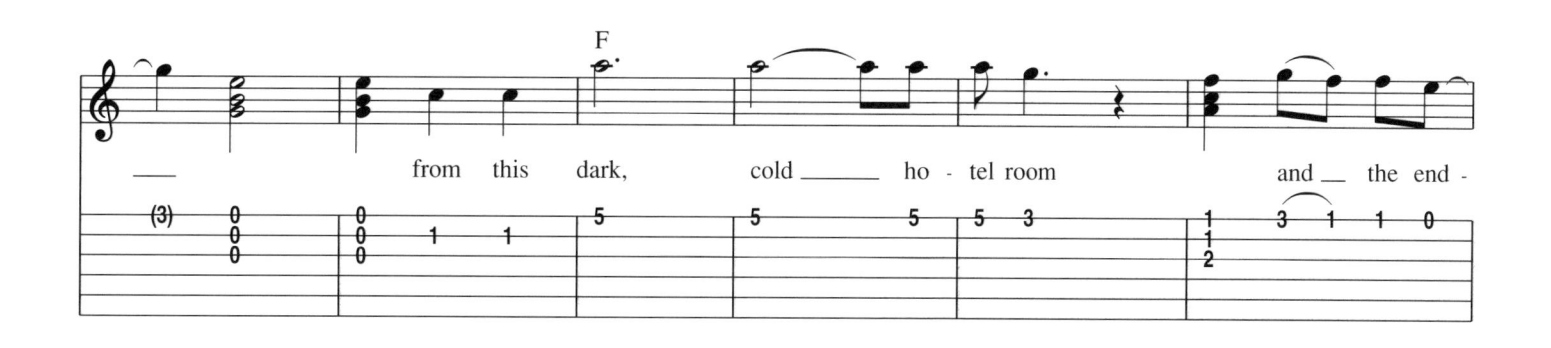

| Dm | | F | |

need some dis - trac - tion oh ____ beau - ti - ful re - lease. ____

| C | Fsus2 | G | Dm |

Mem - o - ry seep from my ____ veins. Let me be emp - ty oh and

| F | | C | Am7 | G7 |

weight - less and may - be I'll find some peace to - night ____ in the

Chorus
| C | | | Em |

arms of the an - gel. Fly a - way ____ from here, ____

| | F | | | |

____ from this dark, cold ____ ho - tel room and ____ the end -

C Am7 G7 G7sus4 C
- less - ness that you fear. You are pulled from the
Em
wreck-age of your si - lent rev - er - ie.
F Fsus4 F
You're in the arms of the an - gel. May you
To Coda
C Am7 G C
find some com - fort here.
D.S. al Coda
F C Fadd9
2. You're so tired of the

Additional Lyrics

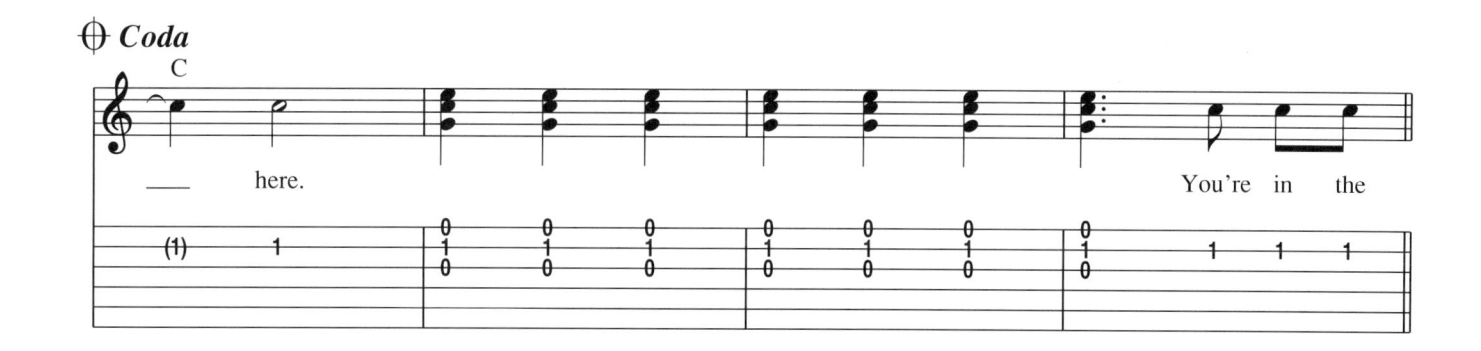

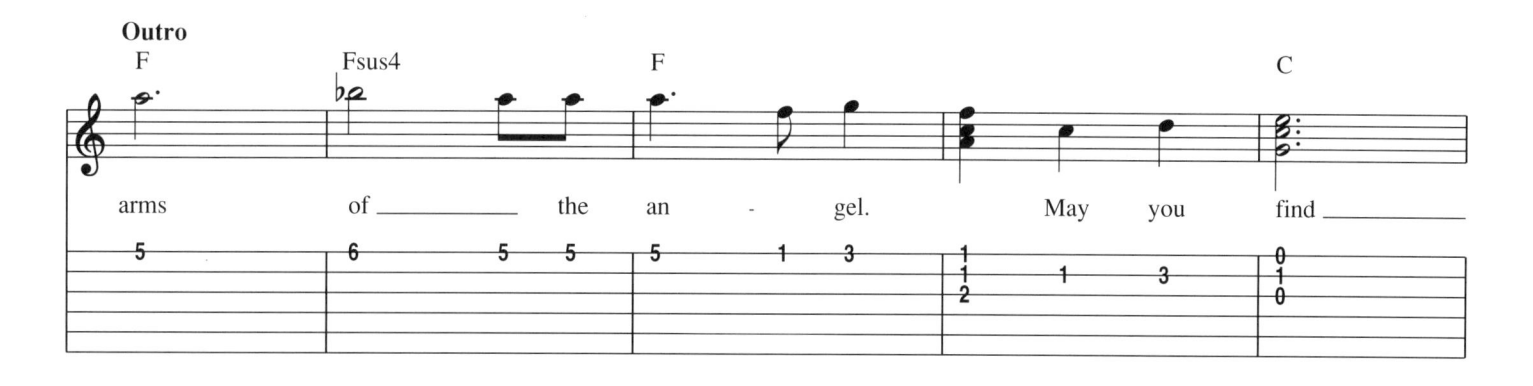

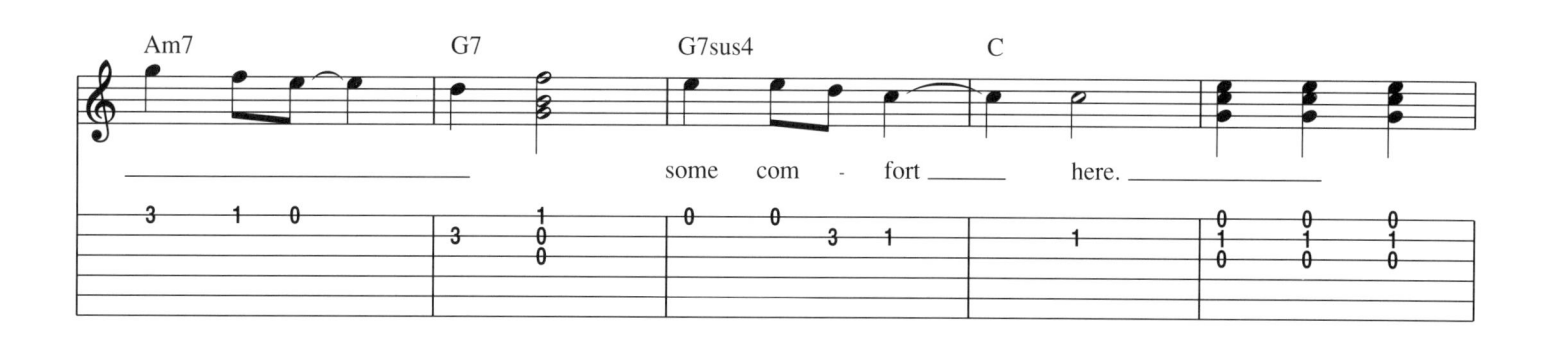

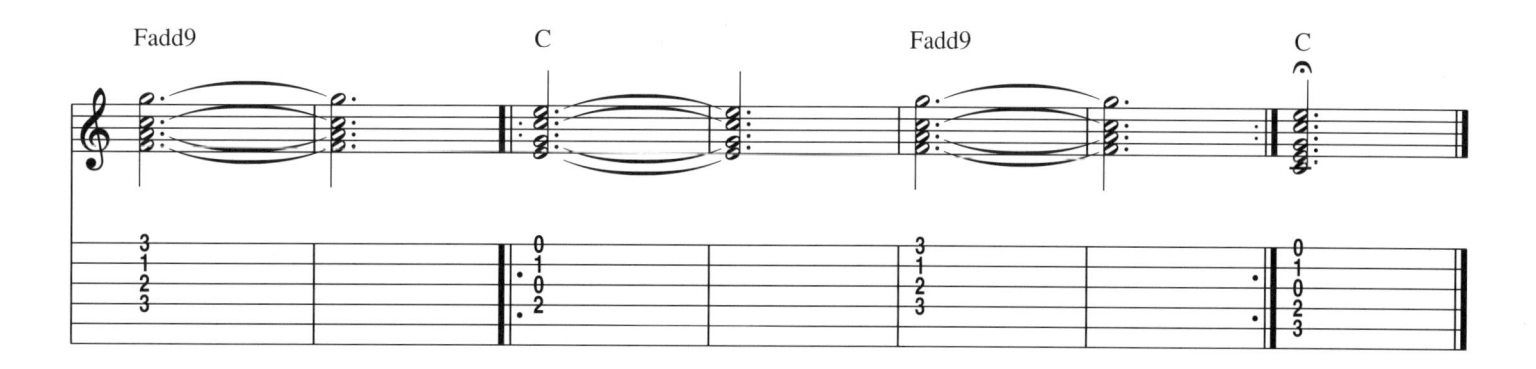

2. You're so tired of the straight line,
   And ev'rywhere you turn
   There's vultures and thieves at your back.
   Storm keeps on twisting.
   Keep on building the lies
   That you make up for all that you lack.
   It don't make no diff'rence
   Escaping one last time.
   It's easier to believe
   In this sweet madness,
   Oh this glorious sadness
   That brings me to my knees

Circle

Words and Music by Sarah McLachlan

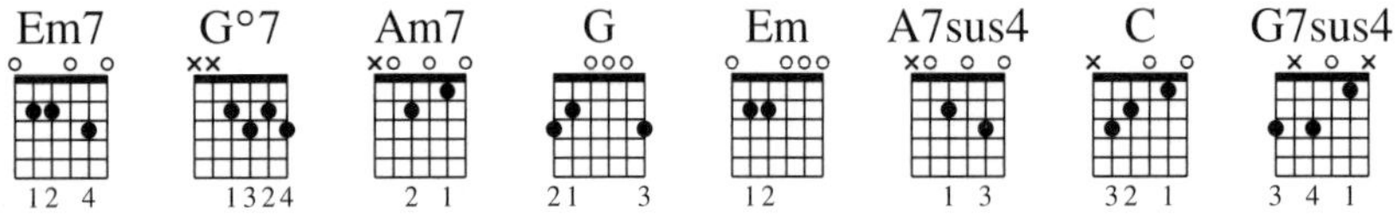

Strum Pattern: 2, 6
Pick Pattern: 2, 4

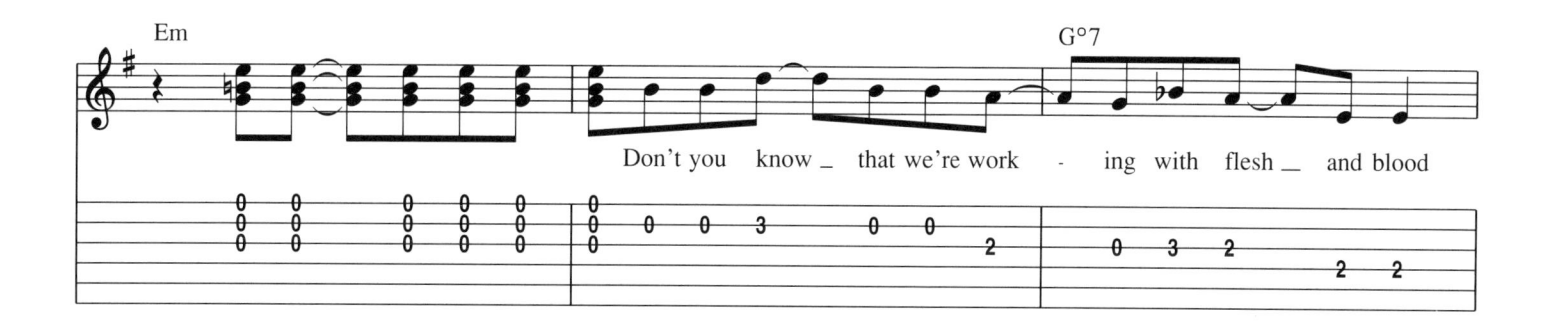

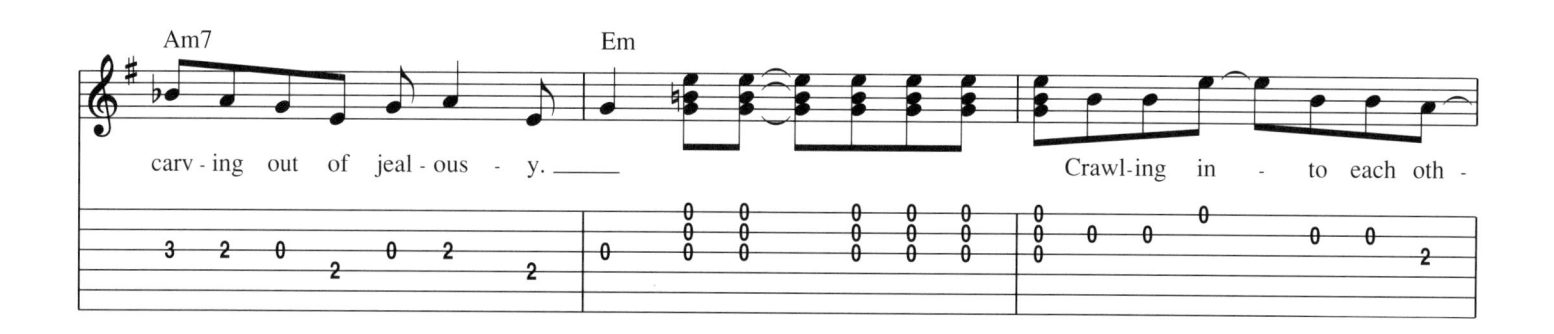

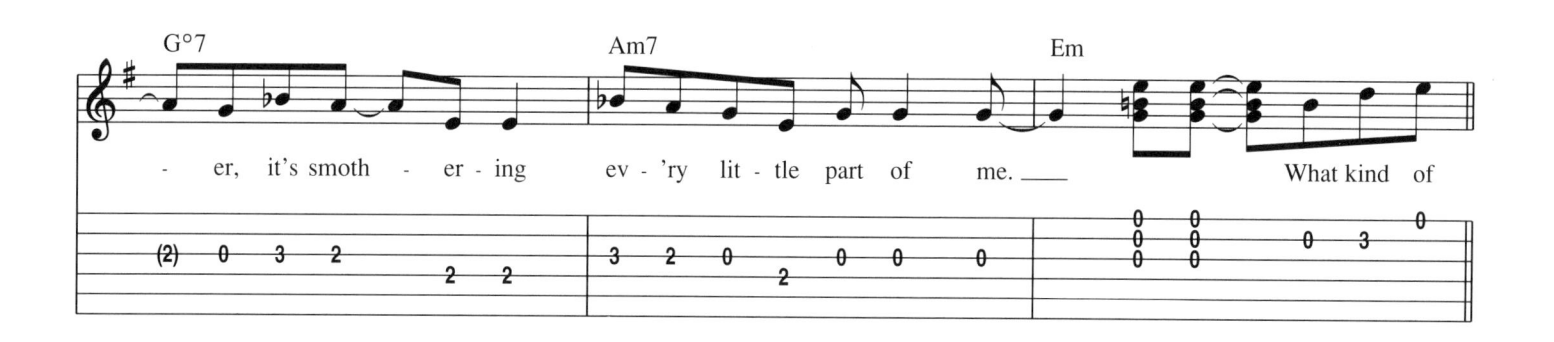

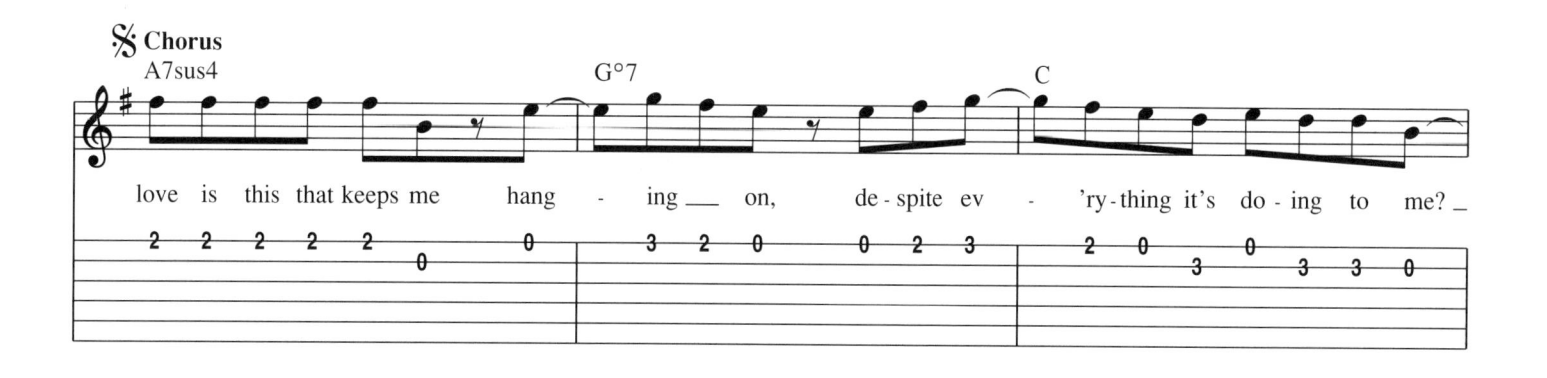

Don't you know that we're working with flesh and blood carving out of jealousy. Crawling into each other, it's smothering ev'ry little part of me. What kind of

Chorus

love is this that keeps me hanging on, despite ev'rything it's doing to me? What is this love that keeps me coming back for more, when it will

Additional Lyrics

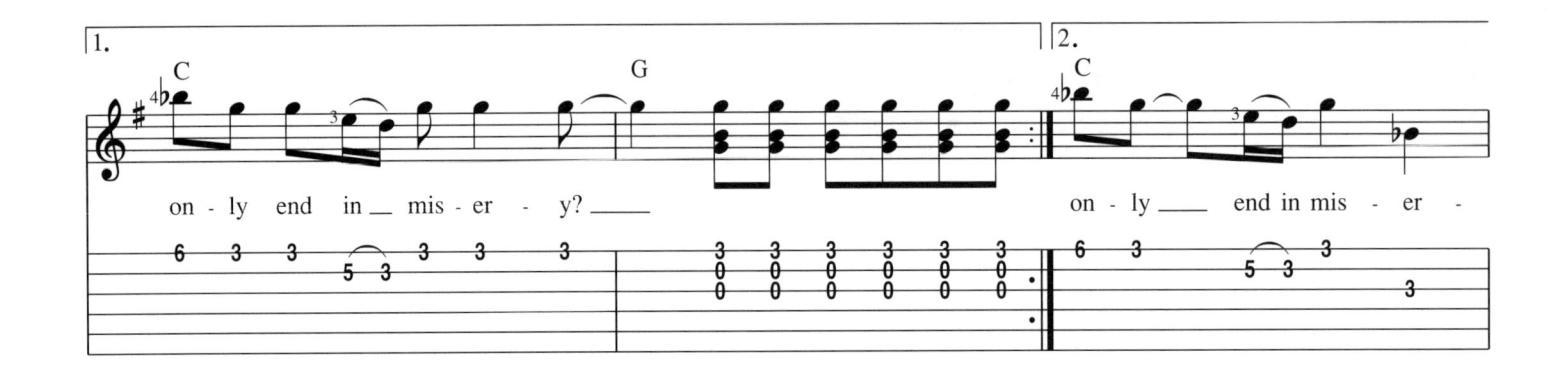

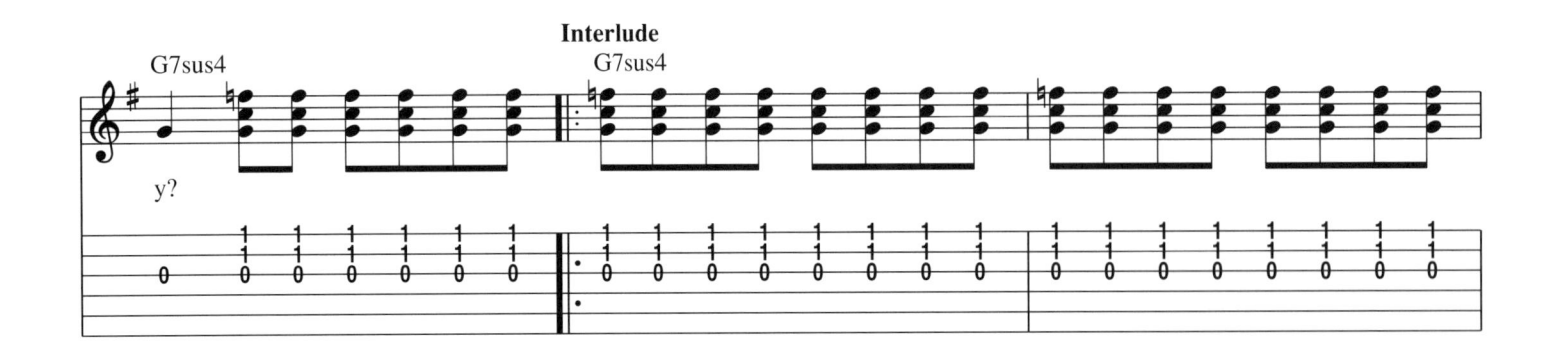

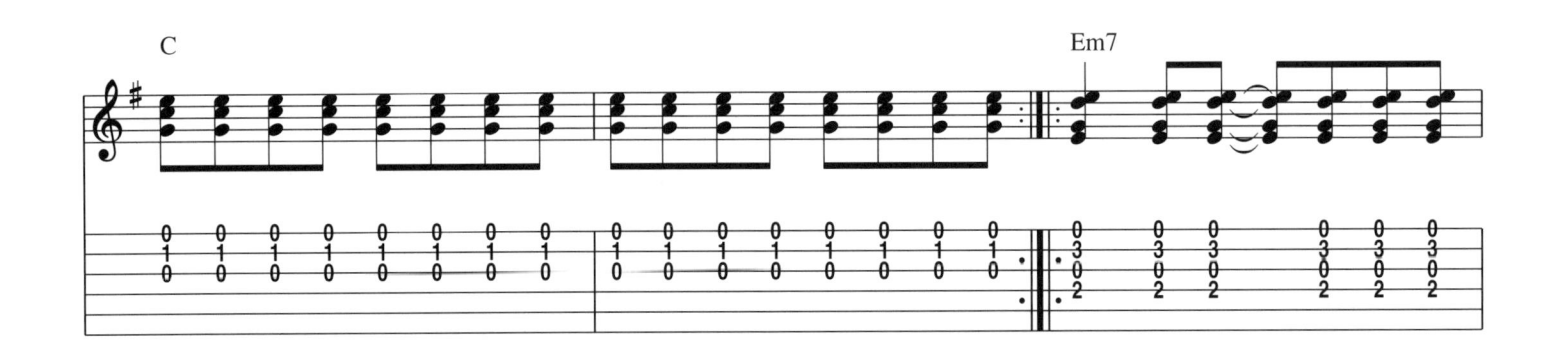

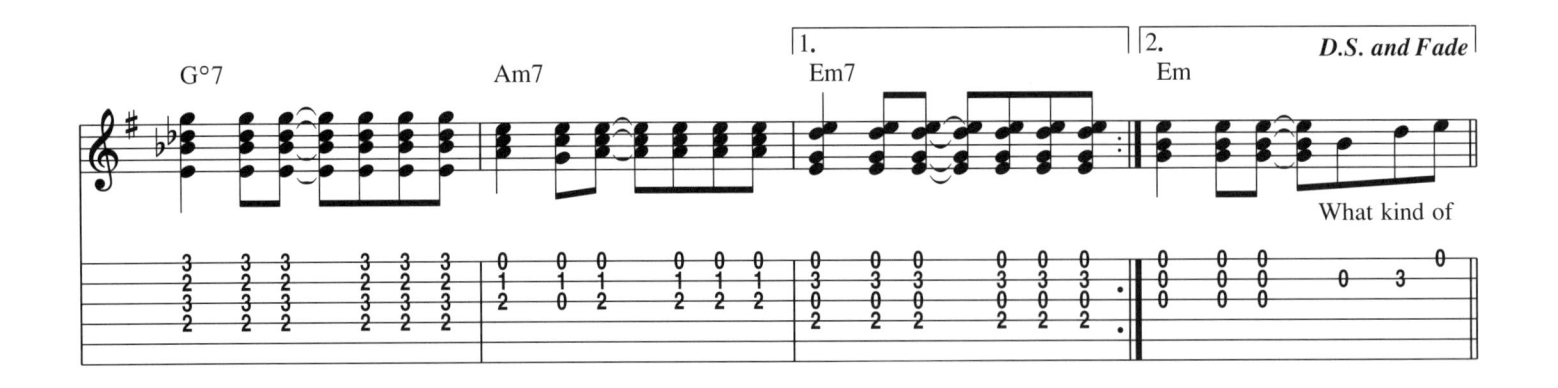

2. I know too many people unhappy
   In a life from which they'd love to flee.
   Watching others get ev'rything offered,
   They're wanton for discovery.
   Oh, my brother, my sister, my mother,
   You're losing your identity.
   Can't you see that it's you in the window,
   Shining with intensity?

Elsewhere

Words and Music by Sarah McLachlan

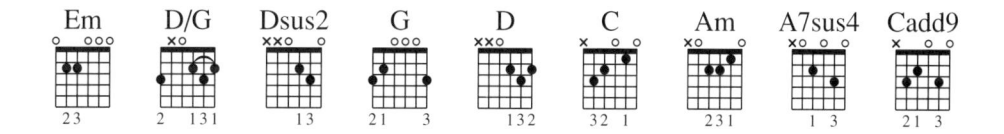

Em   D/G   Dsus2   G   D   C   Am   A7sus4   Cadd9

Strum Pattern: 1, 3
Pick Pattern: 2, 4

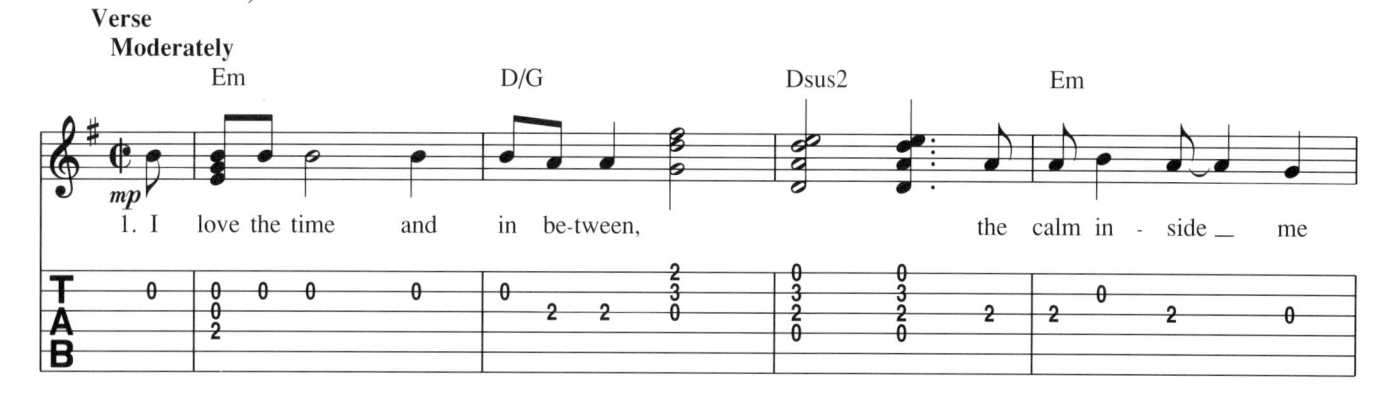

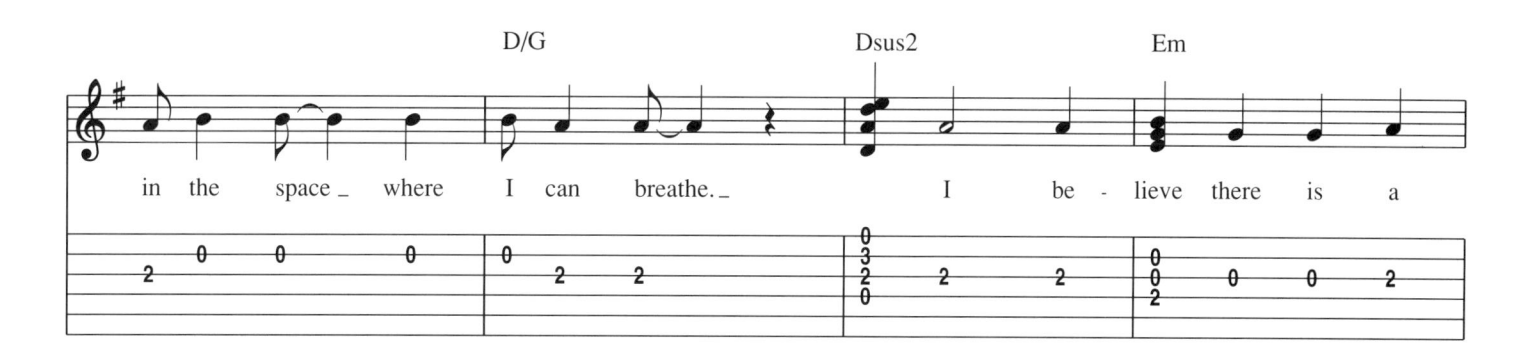

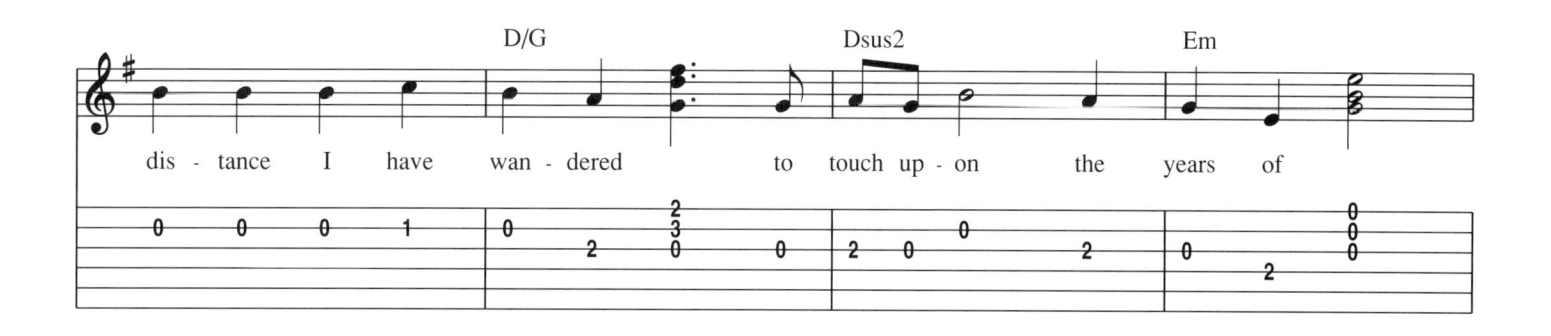

Verse
Moderately

1. I love the time and in be-tween, the calm in-side me in the space where I can breathe. I be-lieve there is a dis-tance I have wan-dered to touch up-on the years of reach-in' out and reach-in' in, hold-

Copyright © 1993 Sony/ATV Songs LLC and Tyde Music
All Rights Administered by Sony/ATV Music Publishing, 8 Music Square West, Nashville, TN 37203
International Copyright Secured   All Rights Reserved

Chorus

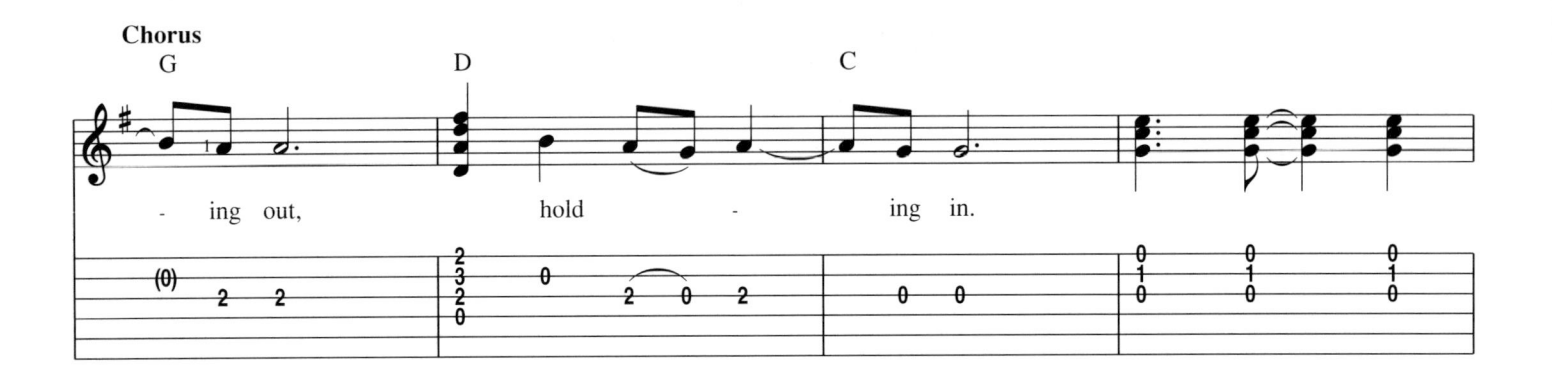

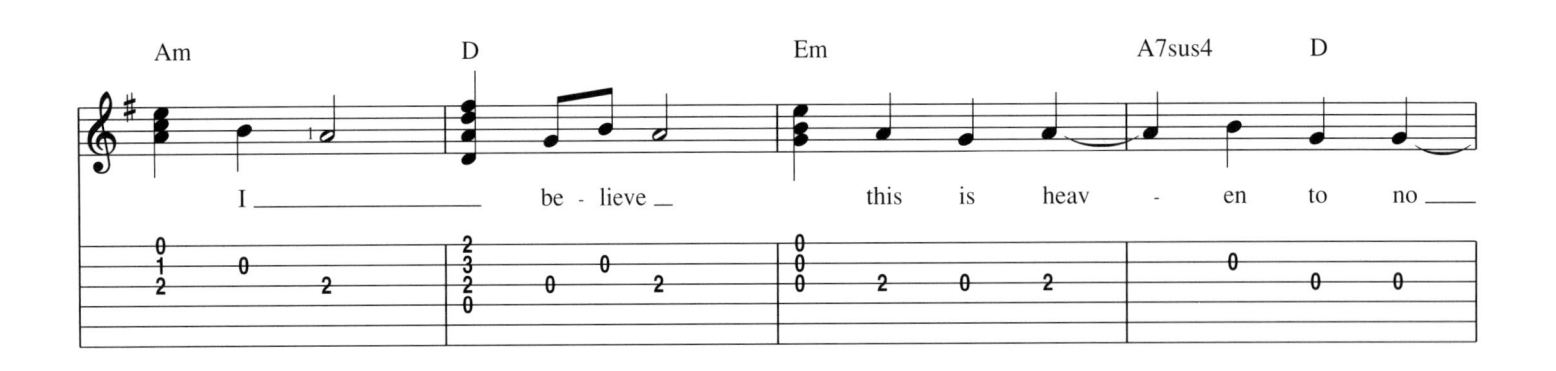

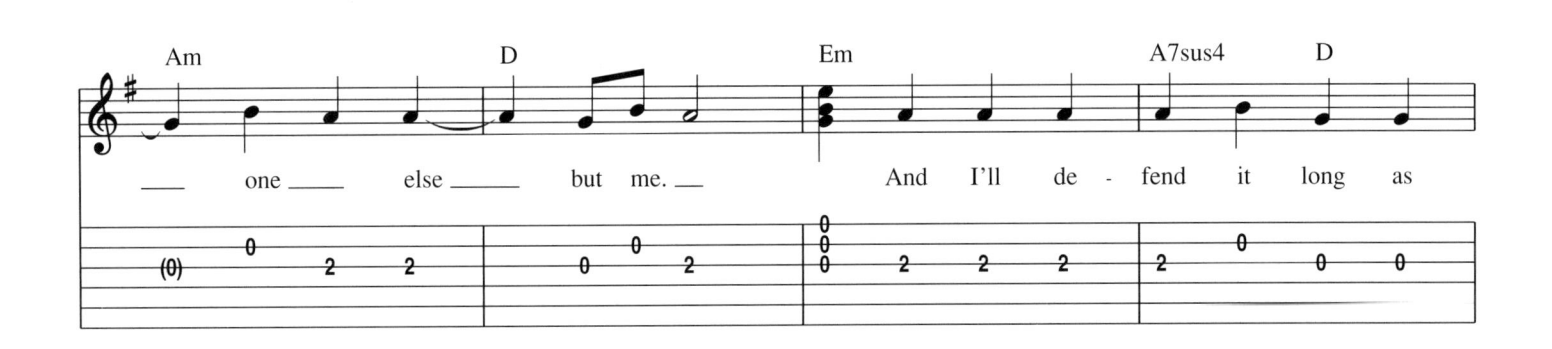

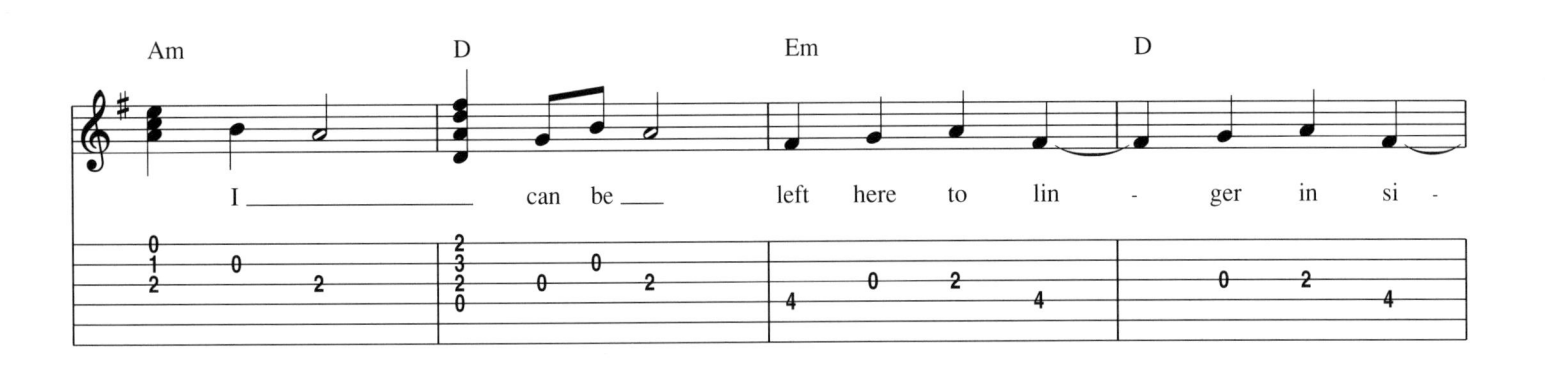

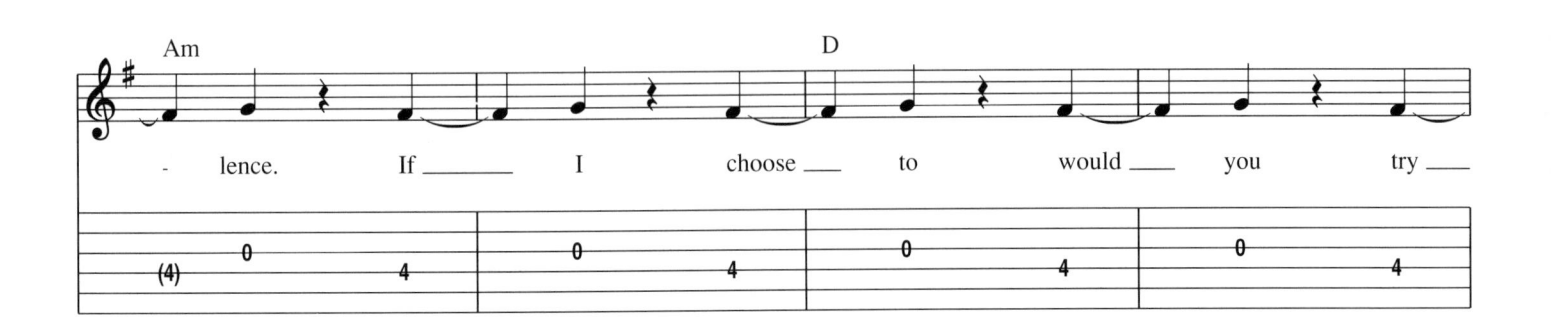

-ing out, holding in.

I believe this is heaven to no one else but me. And I'll defend it long as

I can be left here to linger in si-lence. If I choose to would you try

Am D
to un - der - stand? 2. I
Verse
Em D/G D C
know this love is pass-ing time, pass-ing through like liq - uid.
3. See Additional Lyrics
Em G D Cadd9
I'm drunk in my de - sire. But I
Em G D C
love the way you smile at me. I love the way your hands reach out and
Em G D C
hold me near. I be - lieve
Might not be right for you, but it's

Chorus
G D C Am
right for I, me, oh. I
D Em Am
be - lieve this is heav - en to no one else
D Em Am
but me. And I'll de - fend it long as I
D Em Am
can be left here to lin - ger in si - lence. If
D Am
I choose to, would you try to un -

Additional Lyrics

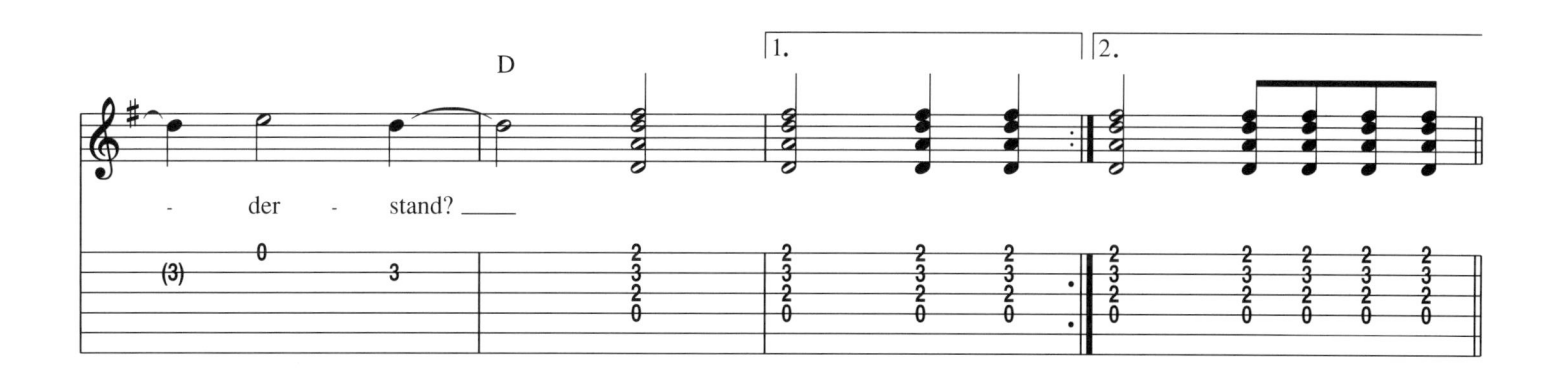

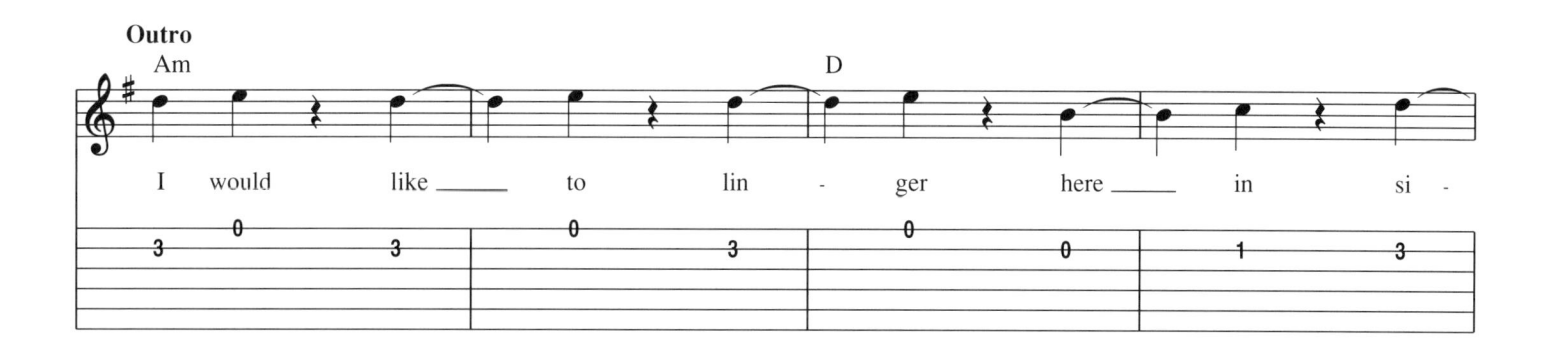

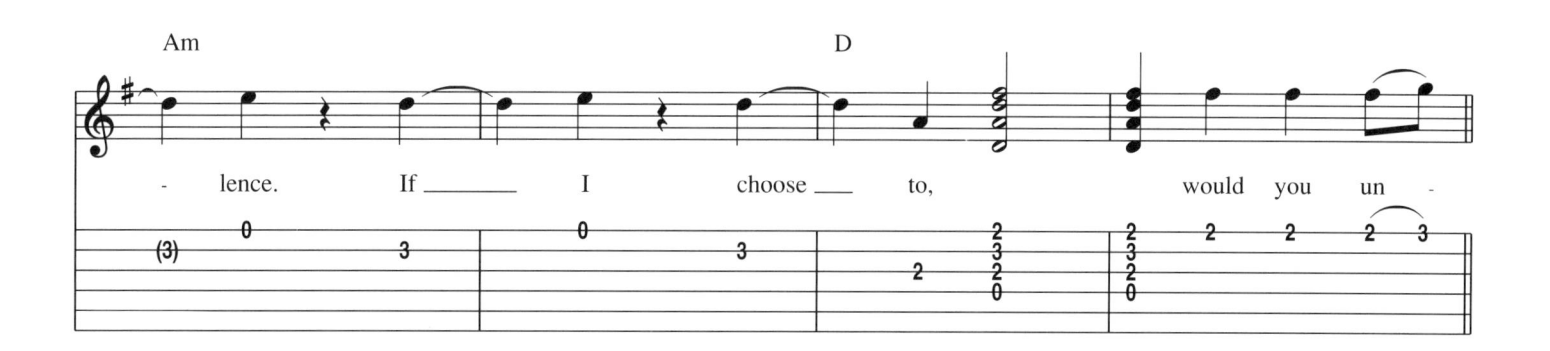

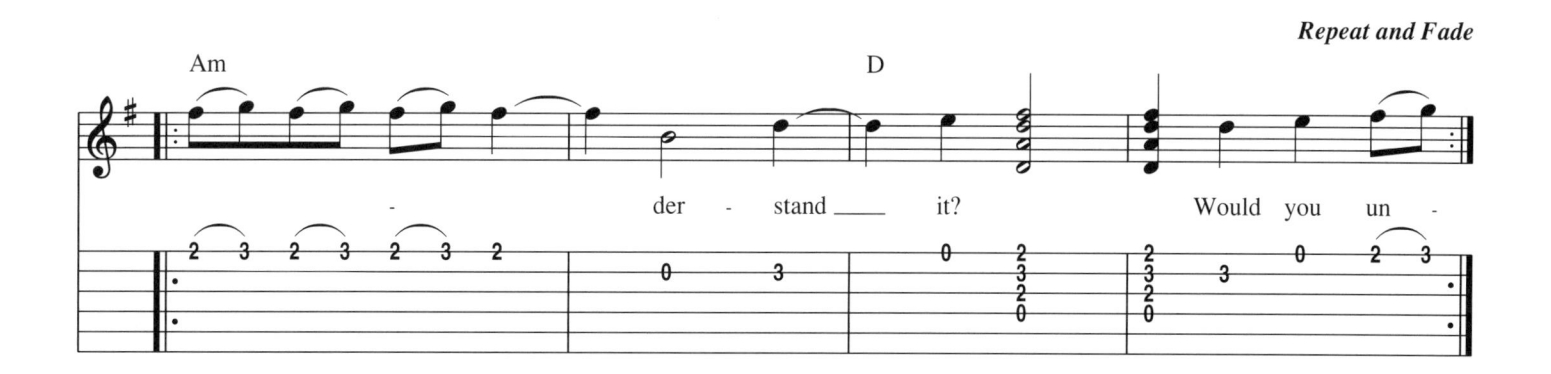

3. Oh, the quiet child awaits the day when
   She can break free the mold that clings like desperation.
   Mother, can't you see I've got to live my life
   The way I feel is right for me?

Do What You Have to Do

Words and Music by Sarah McLachlan and Colleen Wolstenholme

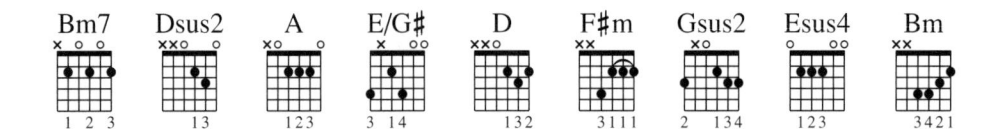

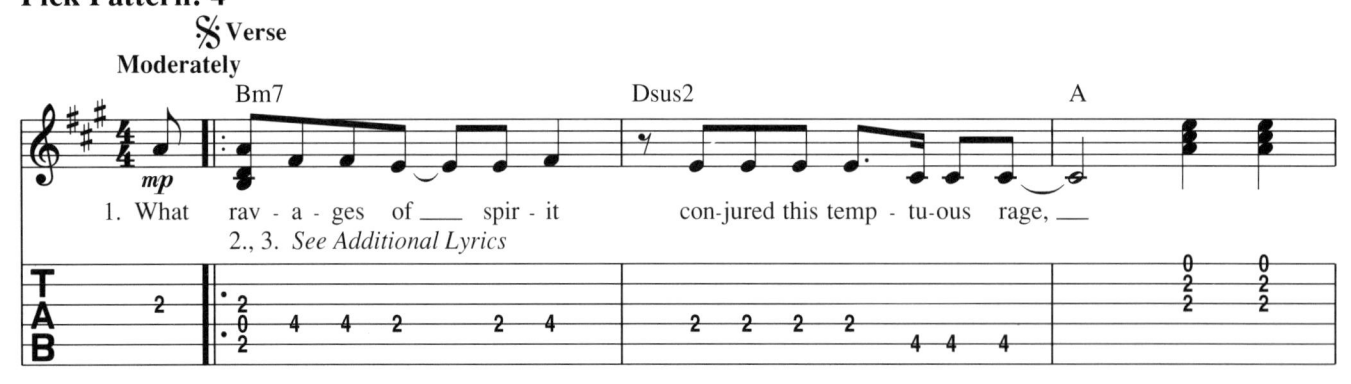

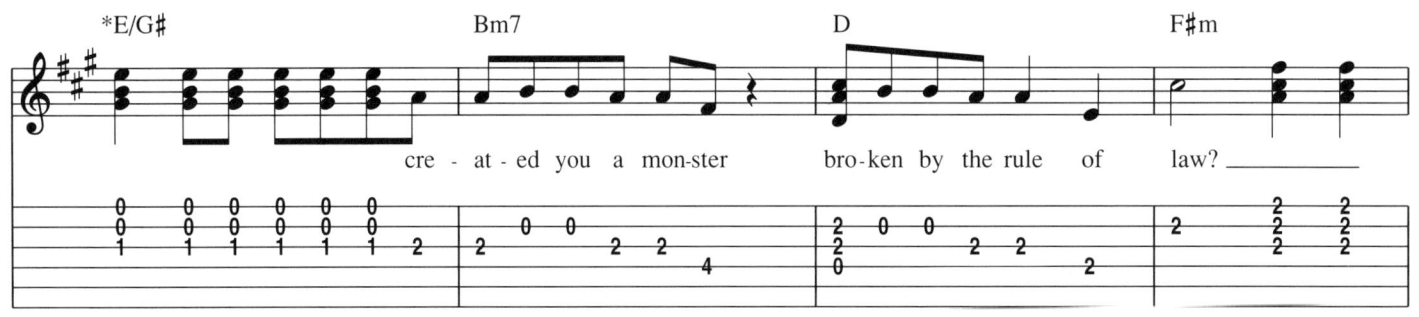

Strum Pattern: 6
Pick Pattern: 4

Verse
Moderately

1. What ravages of ___ spirit conjured this temptuous rage, created you a monster broken by the rule of law? And fate has led you through it. You do what you have to do. ___ And fate has lead you through it. You do what you have to do. ___

2., 3. *See Additional Lyrics*

*2nd time play A.

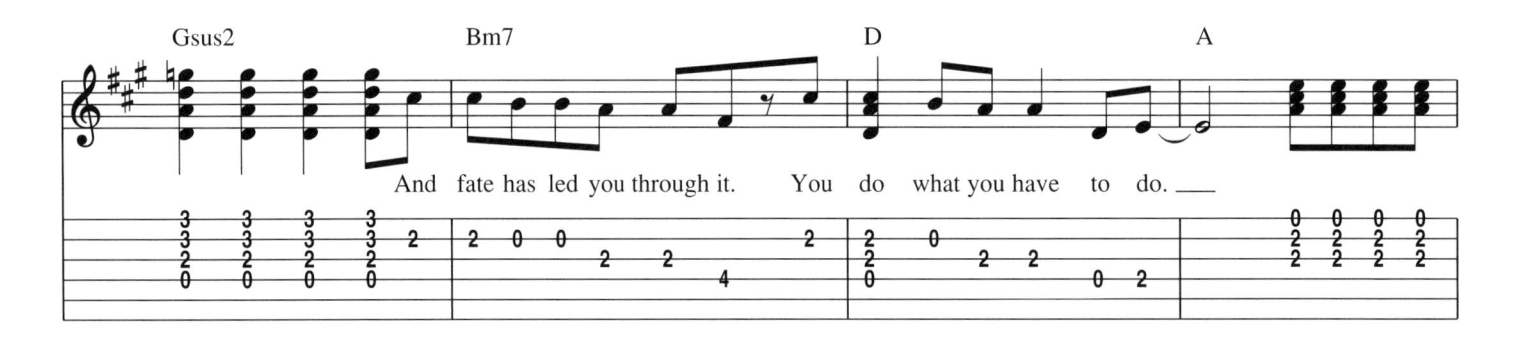

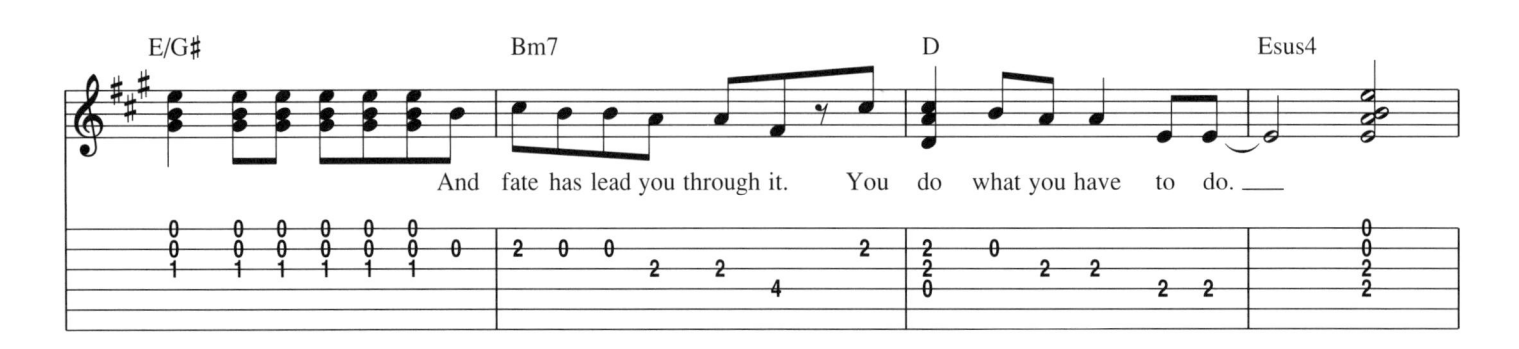

Copyright © 1997 Sony/ATV Songs LLC, Tyde Music and Nettwerk Music Publishing
All Rights on behalf of Sony/ATV Songs LLC and Tyde Music Administered by
Sony/ATV Music Publishing, 8 Music Square West, Nashville, TN 37203
International Copyright Secured   All Rights Reserved

Additional Lyrics

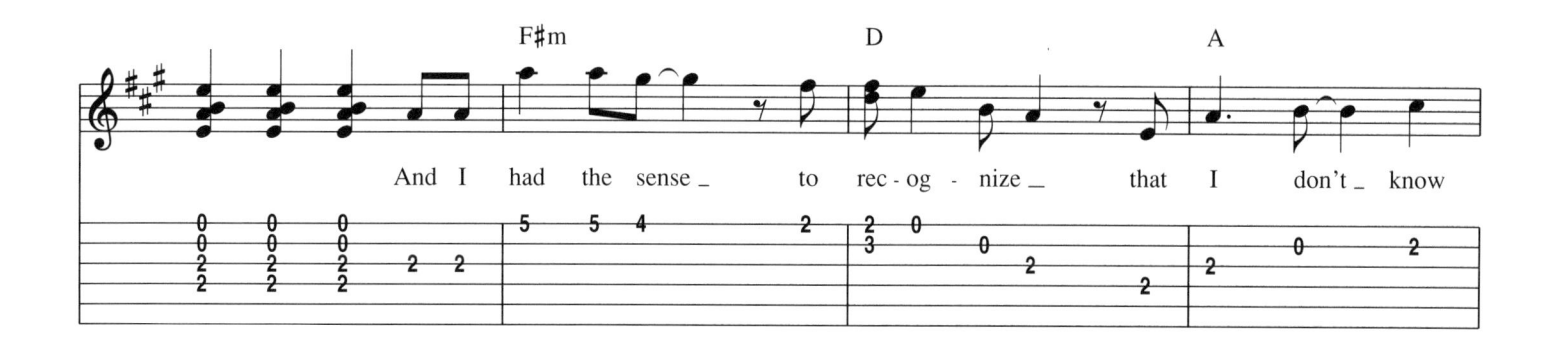

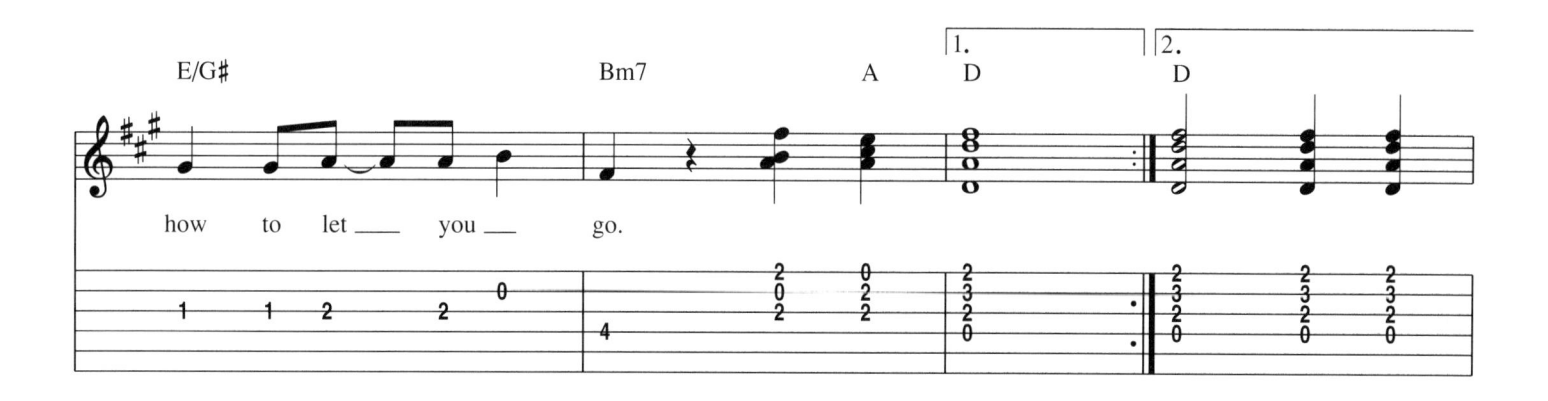

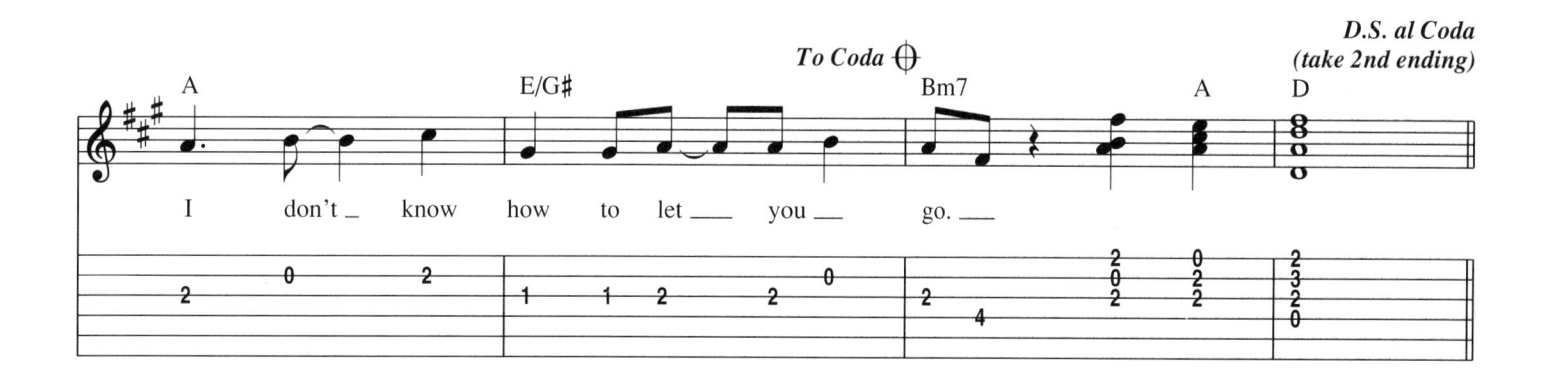

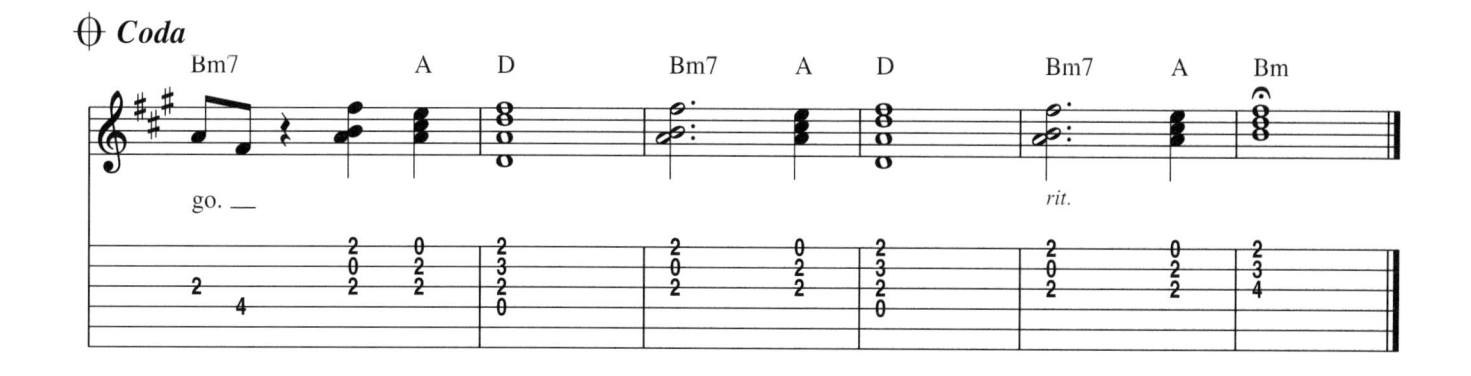

2. Ev'ry moment marked with apparitions of your soul.
   I'm ever swift and moving, try'n' to escape this desire.
   The yearning to be near you, I do what I have to do.
   The yearning to be near you, I do what I have to do.
   And I had the sense to recognize
   That I don't know how to let you go.

3. A glowing ember burning hot and burning slow,
   Deep within I'm shaken by the violence of existing for only you.
   I know I can't be with you, I do what I have to do.
   I know I can't be with you, I do what I have to do.
   And I have the sense to recognize
   But I don't know how to let you go.
   I don't know how to let you go.

Drawn to the Rhythm

Words and Music by Sarah McLachlan

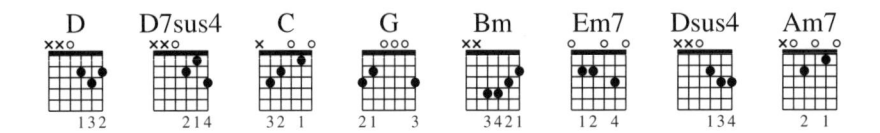

Chords: D D7sus4 C G Bm Em7 Dsus4 Am7

Strum Pattern: 2, 6
Pick Pattern: 4, 6

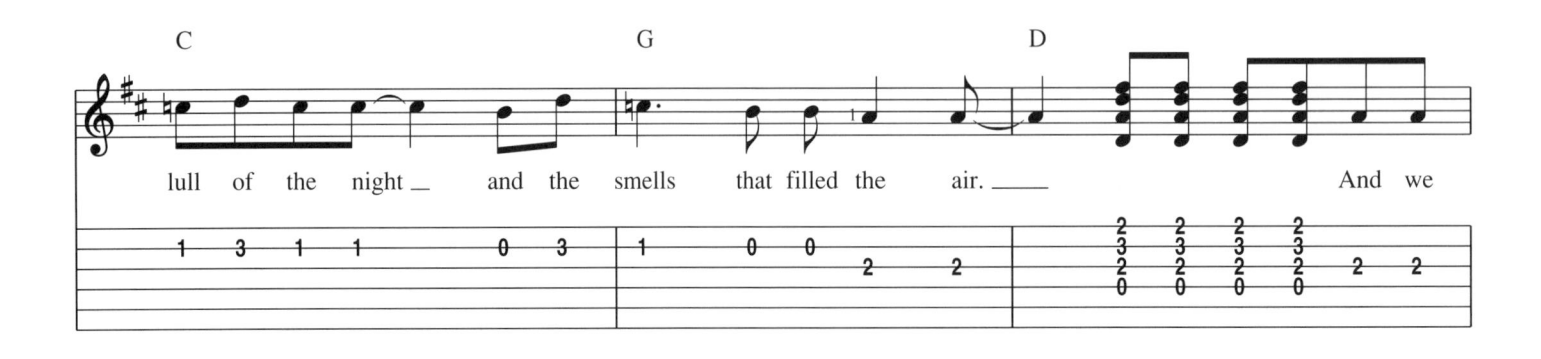

Verse
Moderately

1. When we were a heart of stone, we wandered to the sea, hoping to find some comfort there, yearning to feel free. And we were mesmerized by the lull of the night and the smells that filled the air. And we

© Copyright 1991 by MUSIC CORPORATION OF AMERICA, INC. and NETTOVERBOARD PUBLISHING LTD.
All Rights Controlled and Administered by MUSIC CORPORATION OF AMERICA, INC.
International Copyright Secured   All Rights Reserved
MCA Music Publishing

27

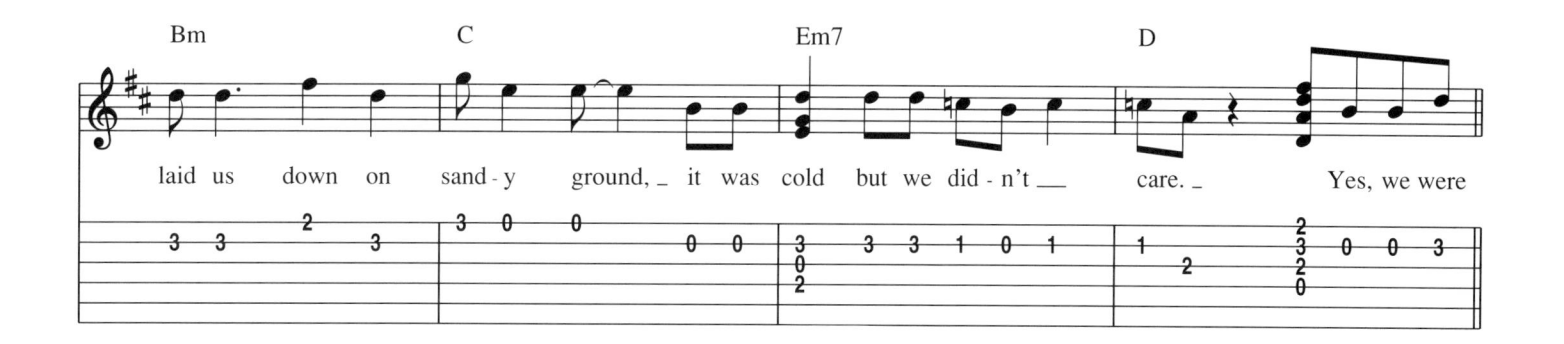

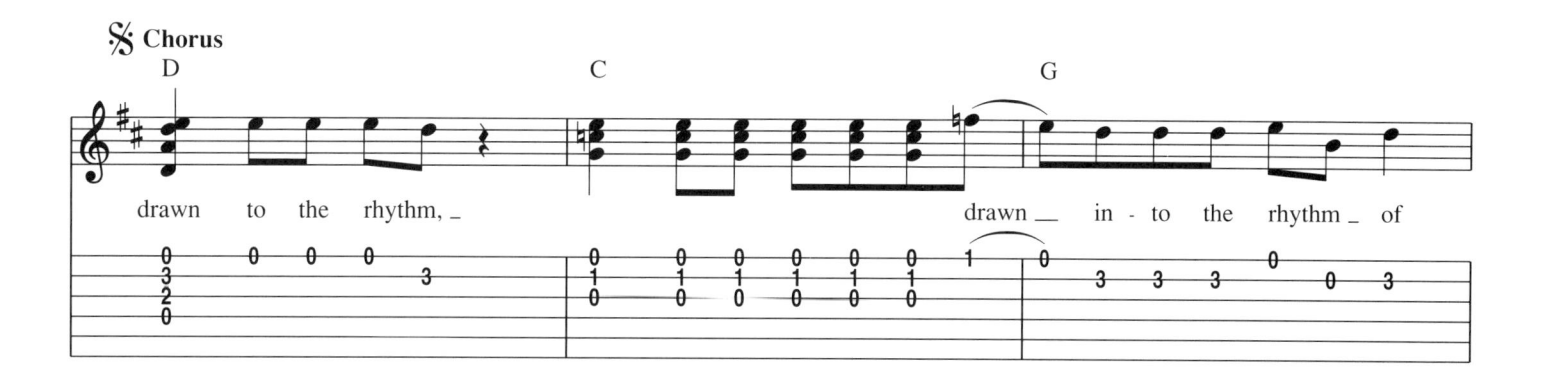

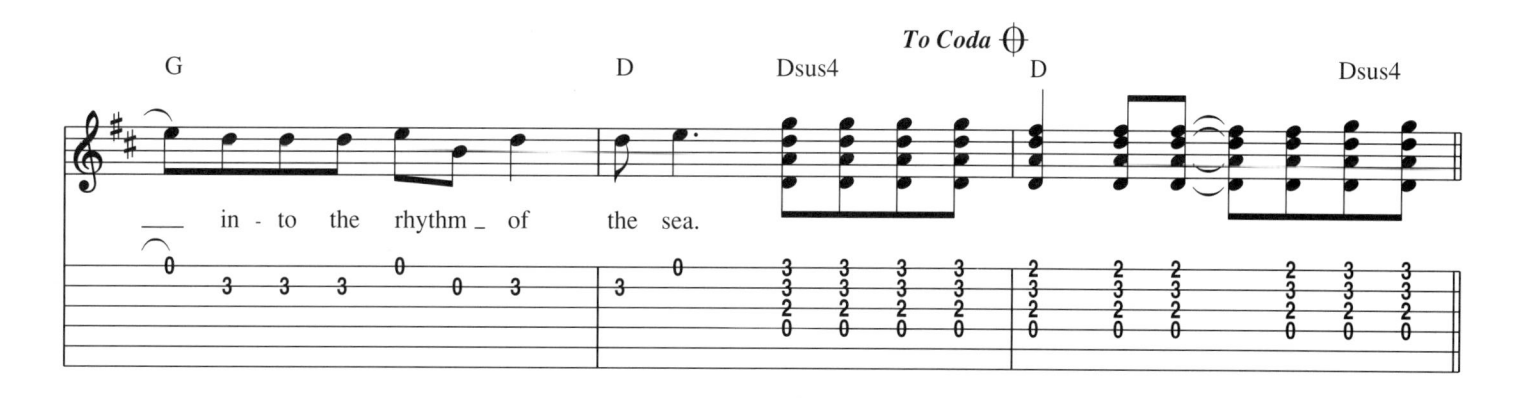

D Bm C
night. Mem - 'ries stirred in - side of us; the
G D Bm
strug - gle and the fight. And we could feel the heat of a thou -
C Em7 D Dsus4 D
- sand voic - es tell - ing us which way to go. And we cried out, is there
D.S. al Coda
Am7 G D Dsus4
no es - cape from the words that plague me so. And we were
Coda
Interlude
D Dsus4 D Dsus4
Verse
Bm
3. In the still and the

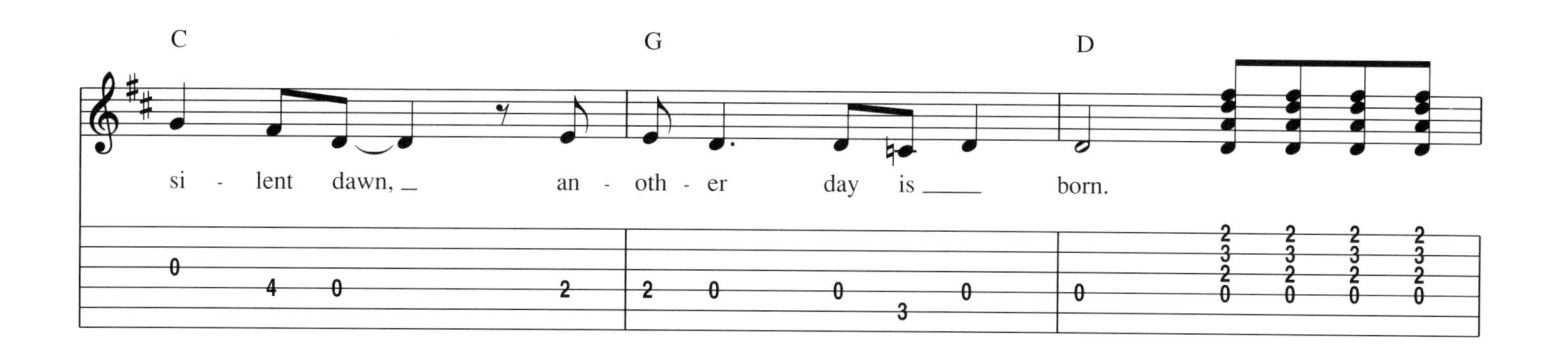

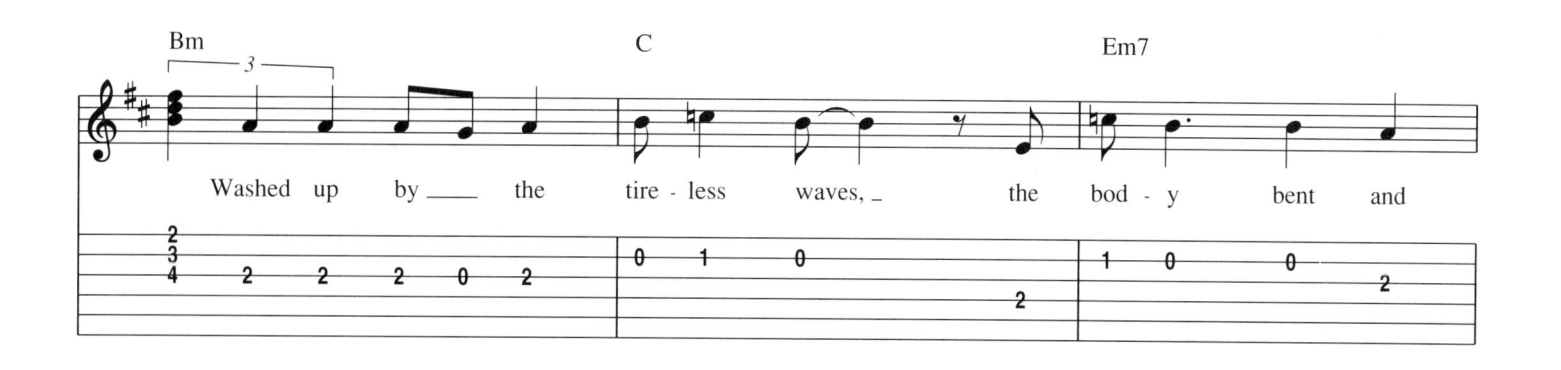

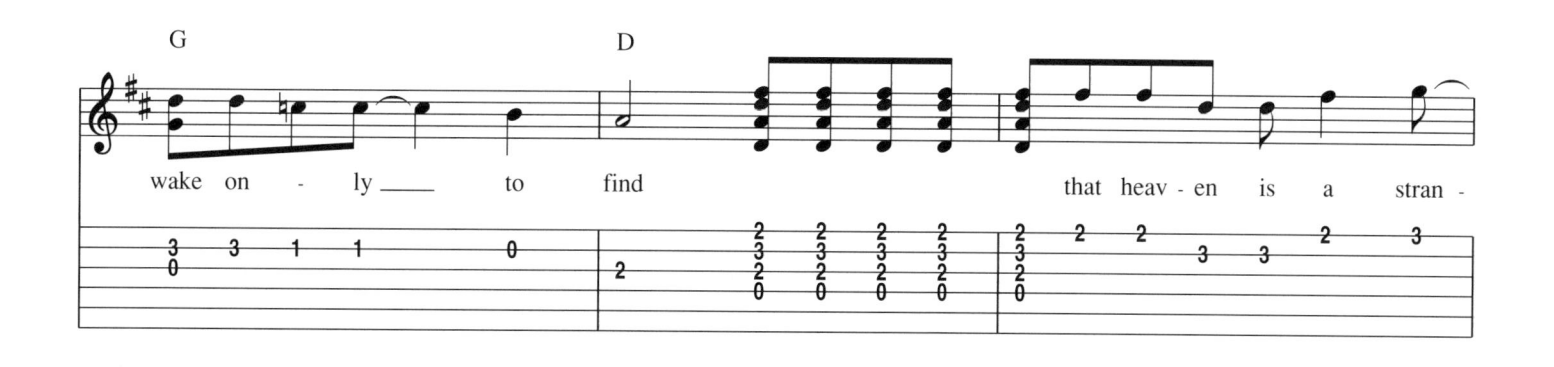

silent dawn, _ an - oth - er day is _ born. Washed up by _ the tire - less waves, _ the bod - y bent and torn. In the face _ of the blind - ing sun, _ a - wake on - ly _ to find that heav - en is a stran - ger place then the one I've left _ be - hind. And we are

D.S. and Fade

Good Enough

Words and Music by Sarah McLachlan

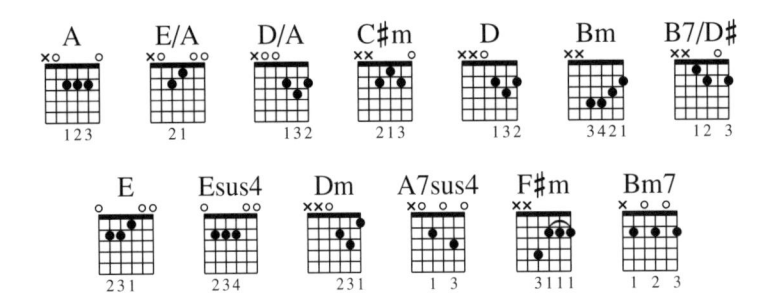

Chords: A, E/A, D/A, C#m, D, Bm, B7/D#, E, Esus4, Dm, A7sus4, F#m, Bm7

Strum Pattern: 1, 2
Pick Pattern: 2, 4

Verse
Moderately

1. Hey, your glass is empty; it's a hell of a long way home. Why don't you let me take you; it's no good to go alone.
2. *See Additional Lyrics*

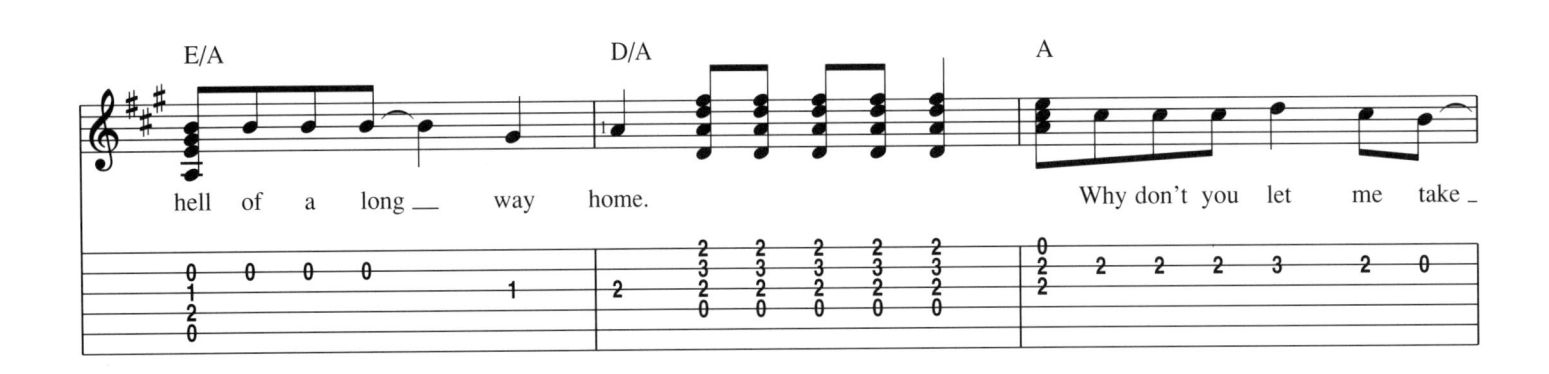

Copyright © 1993 Sony/ATV Songs LLC and Tyde Music
All Rights Administered by Sony/ATV Music Publishing, 8 Music Square West, Nashville, TN 37203
International Copyright Secured All Rights Reserved

31

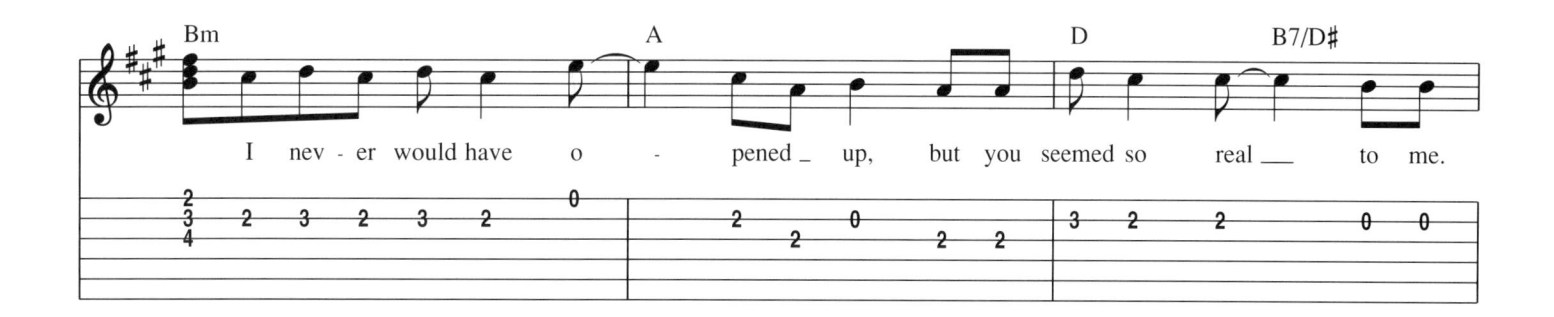

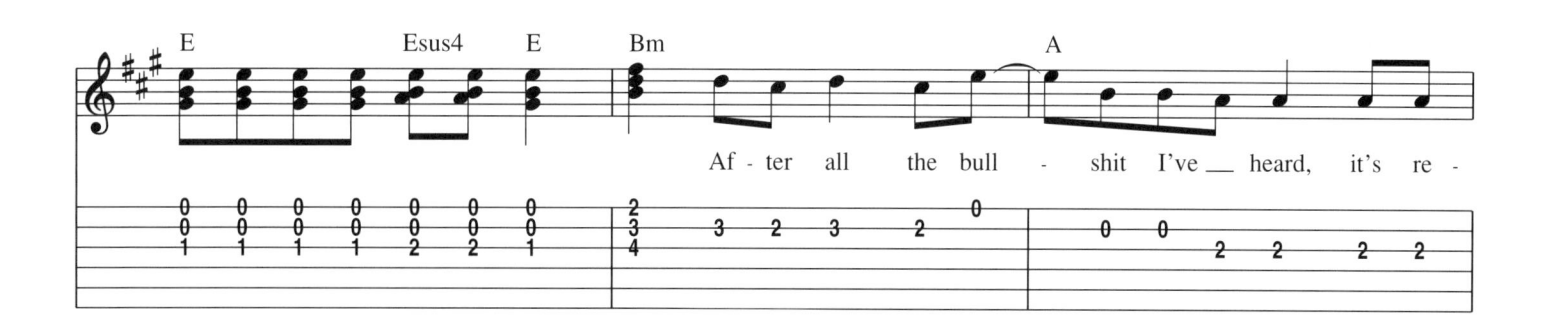

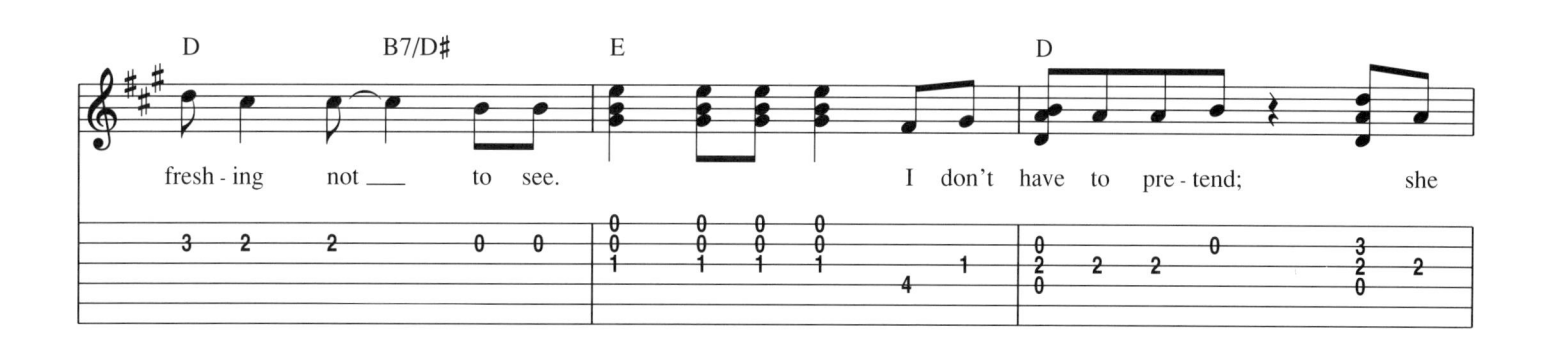

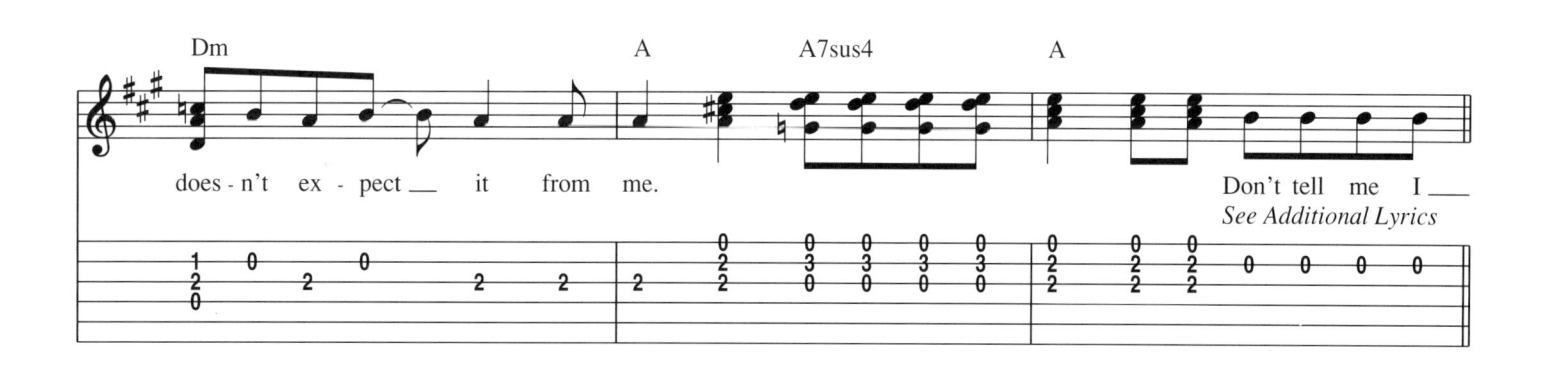

F♯m D A E
for you. Just tell me why nothing is good e-nough.
1. 2.
Esus4 E D
Oh, so just let me try and I will be good
F♯m D F♯m
to you. Just let me try and I will be there for you. I'll show you why
Interlude
Bm7 A E E
you're so much more than good e-nough.
A F♯m D E
1. So, don't tell me why

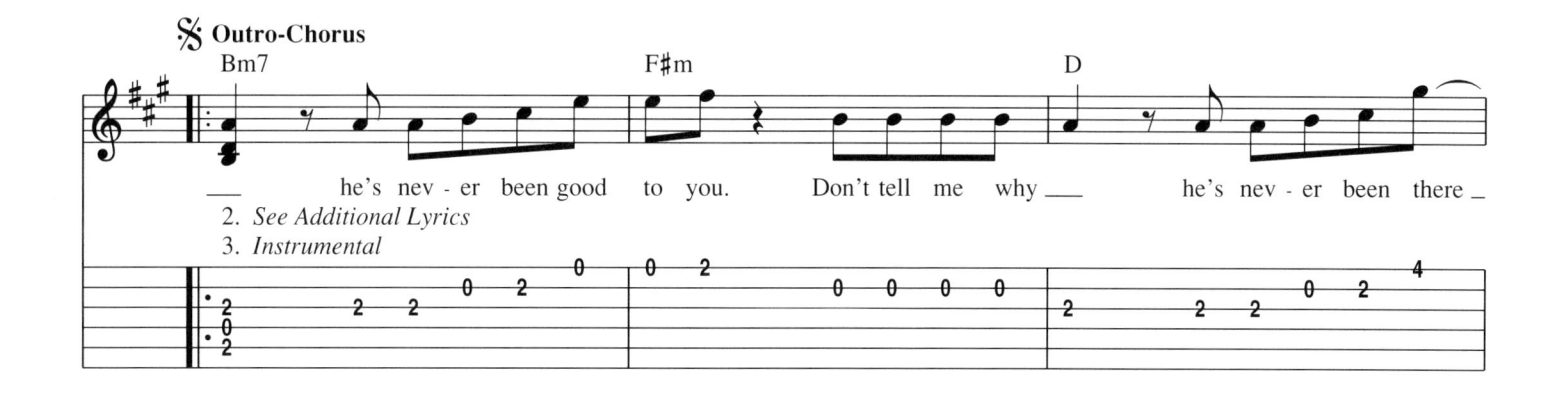

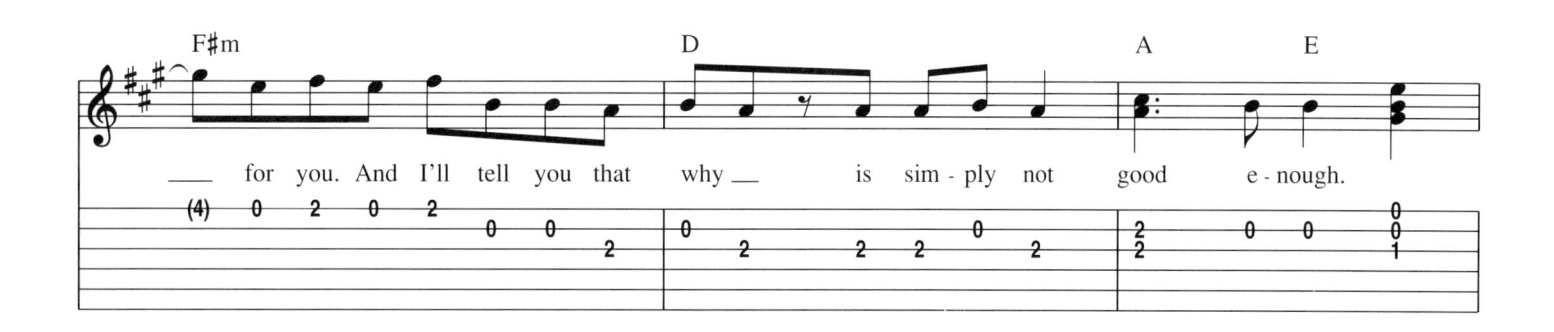

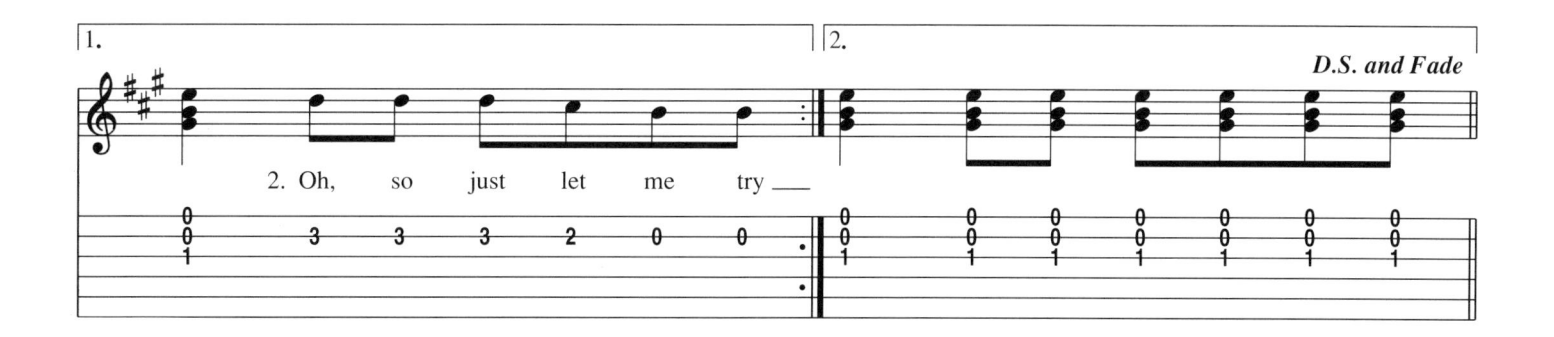

Outro-Chorus

he's never been good to you. Don't tell me why he's never been there for you. And I'll tell you that why is simply not good enough.

1.
2. Oh, so just let me try

D.S. and Fade

Additional Lyrics

2. Hey, little girl, would you like some candy?
   Your momma said that it's okay.
   The door is open, come on outside.
   No, I can't come out today.
   It's not the wind that cracked
   Your shoulder and threw you to the ground.
   Who's there that makes you so afraid.
   Your shaken to the bone. You know I don't understand;
   You deserve so much more than this.

Chorus So, don't tell me why he's never been good to you.
   Don't tell me why he's never been there for you.
   And I'll tell you that why is simply not good enough.
   Oh, so just let me try and I will be good to you.
   Just let me try and I will be there for you.
   I'll show you why you're so much more than good enough.

Outro-Chorus 2. Oh, so just let me try and I will be good to you.
   Just let me try and I will be there for you.
   I'll show you why you're so much more than good enough.

33

Hold On

Words and Music by Sarah McLachlan

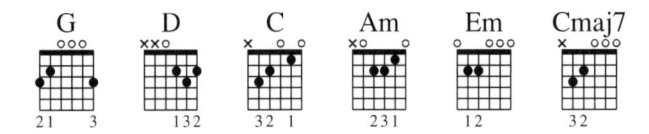

Chords: G, D, C, Am, Em, Cmaj7

Strum Pattern: 1, 2
Pick Pattern: 2, 4

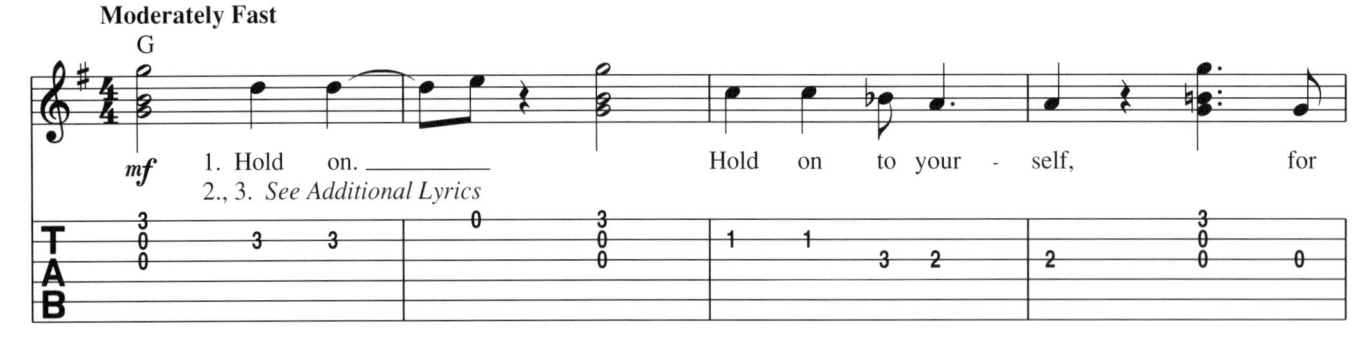

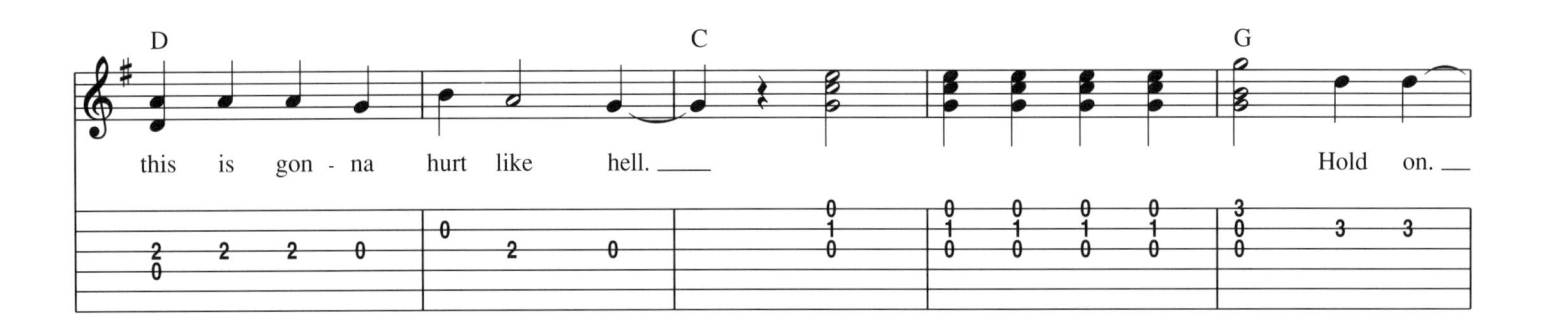

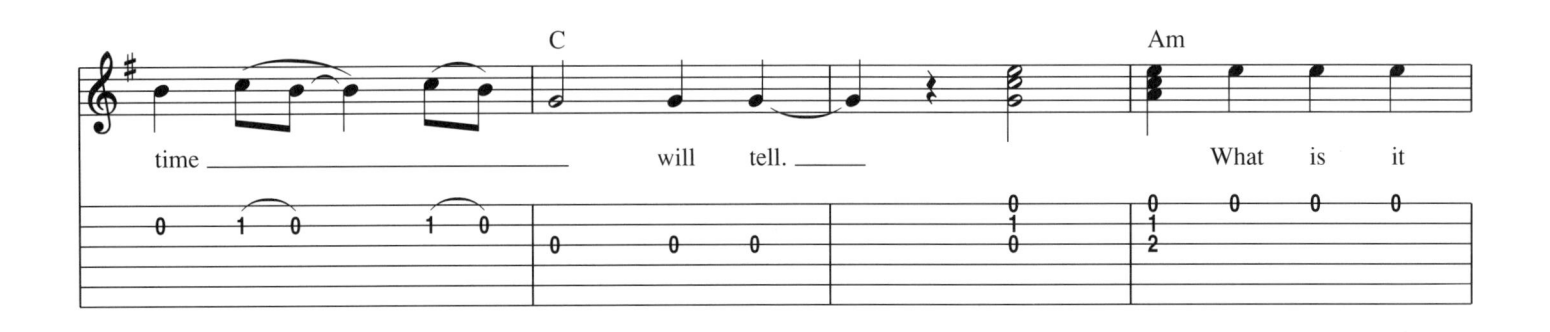

Verse
Moderately Fast

1. Hold on. Hold on to yourself, for
2., 3. *See Additional Lyrics*

this is gonna hurt like hell. Hold on.

Hold on to yourself. You know that only

time will tell. What is it

Copyright © 1993 Sony/ATV Songs LLC and Tyde Music
All Rights Administered by Sony/ATV Music Publishing, 8 Music Square West, Nashville, TN 37203
International Copyright Secured   All Rights Reserved

35

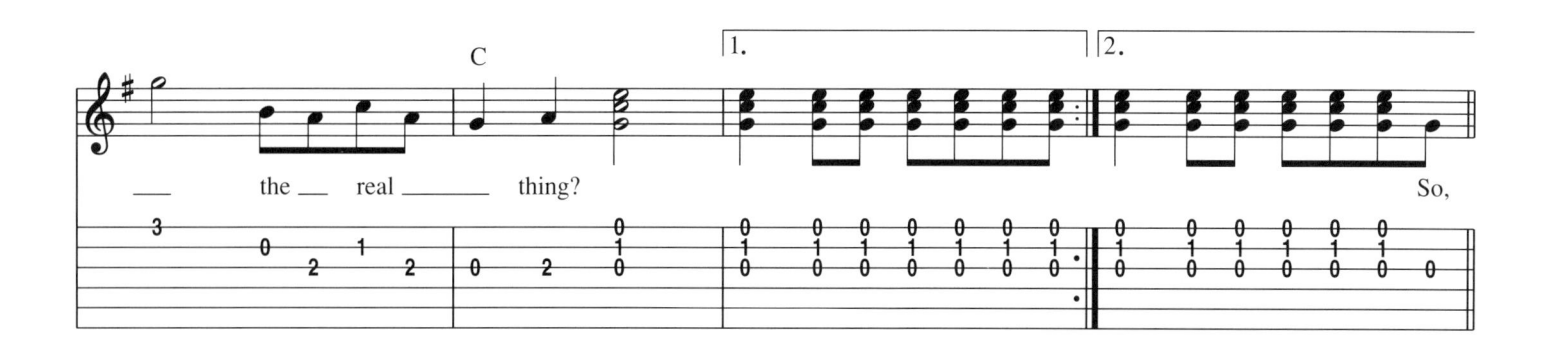

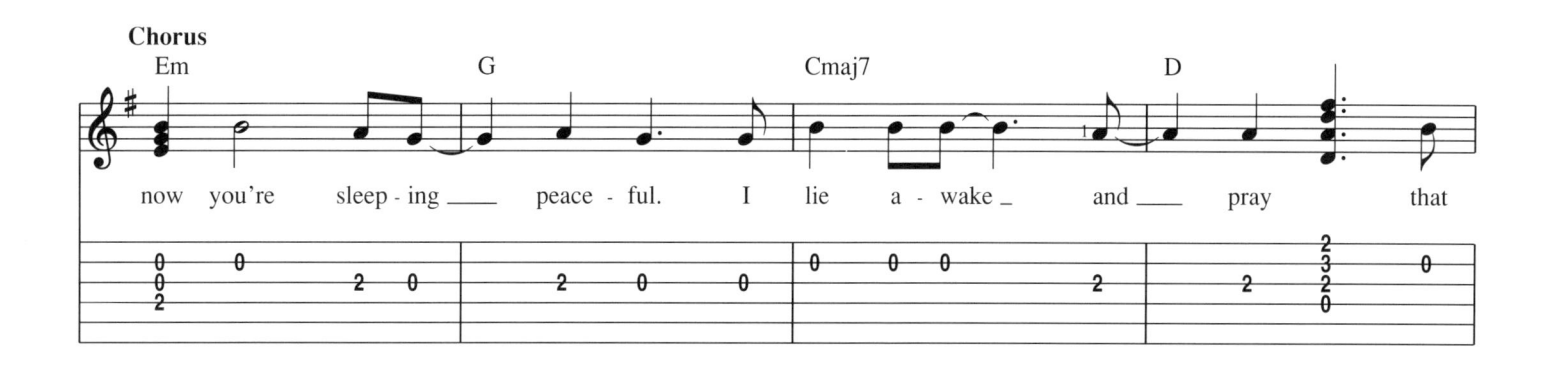

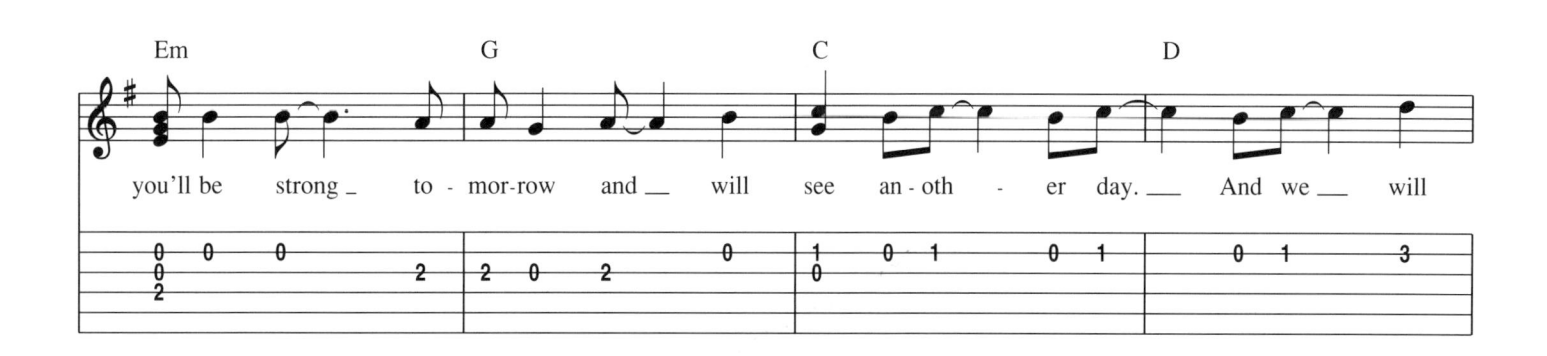

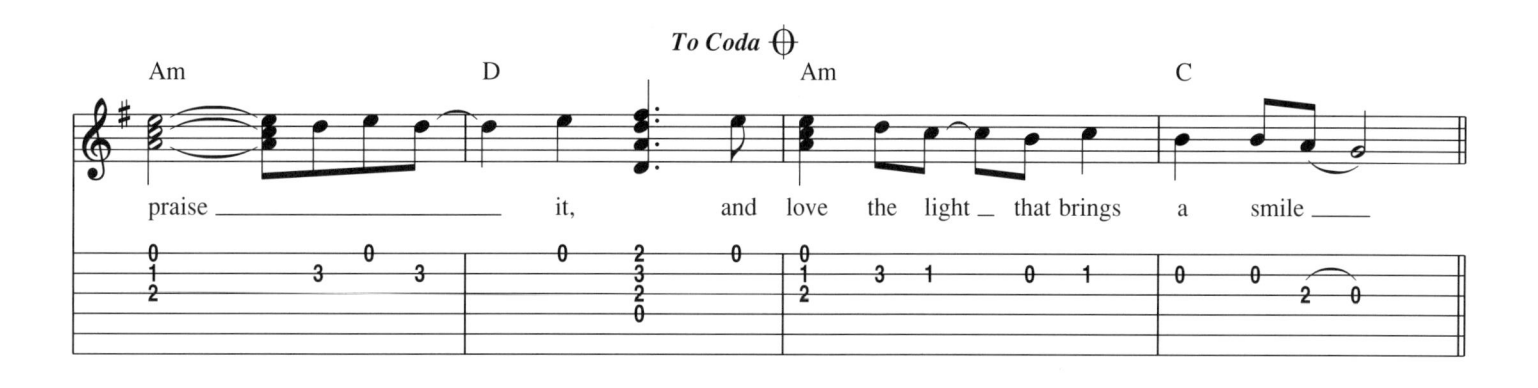

Additional Lyrics

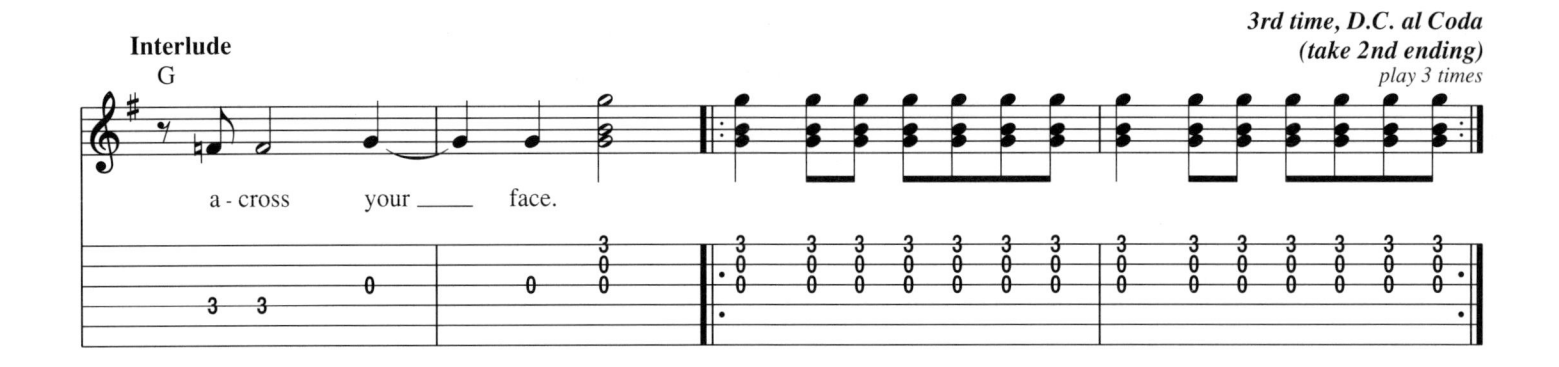

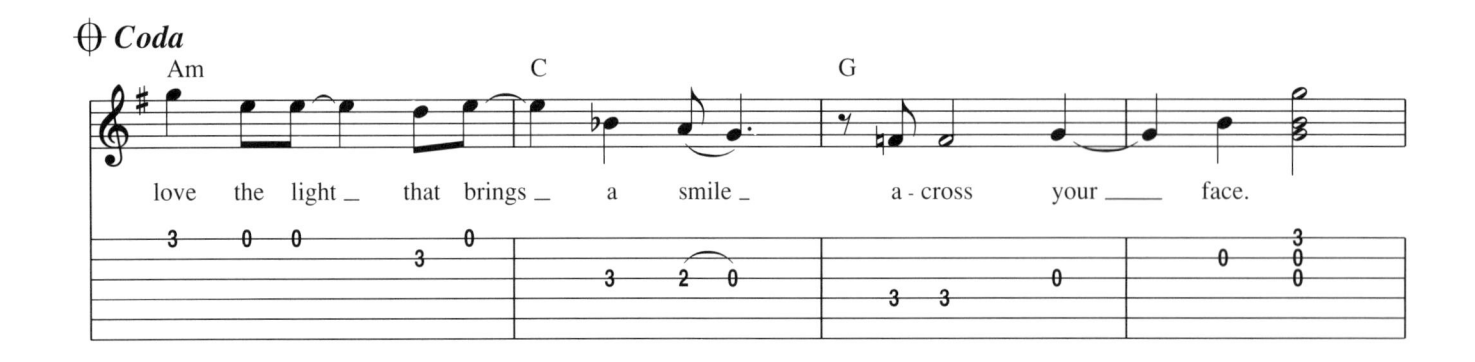

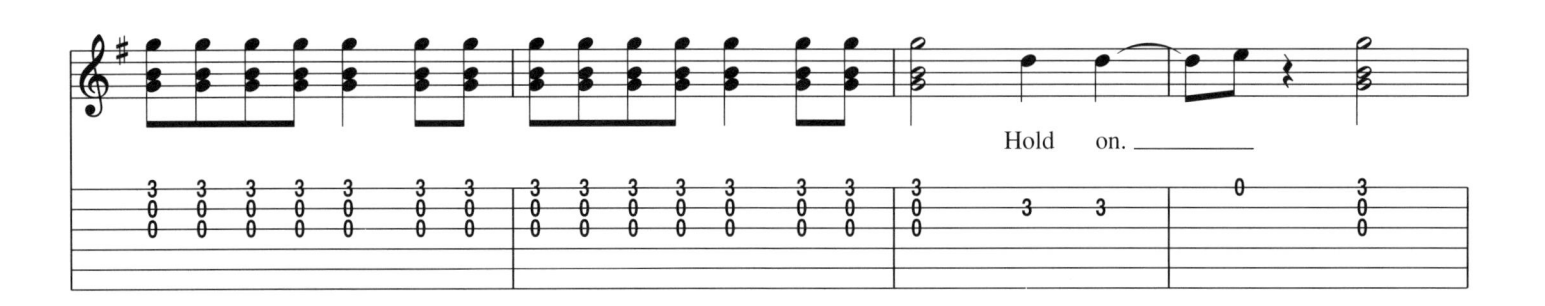

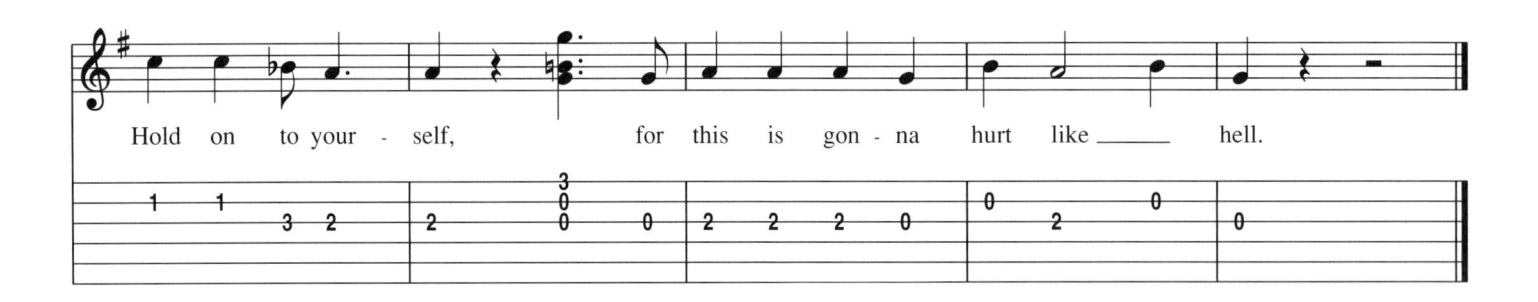

2. My love, you know that you're my best friend.
   You know that I'd do anything for you.
   My love, let nothing come between us.
   My love for you is strong and true.
   Am I in heaven here or am I...
   At the crossroads I am standing.

3. Oh God, if You're out there, won't You hear me?
   I know we've never talked before.
   Oh God, the man I love is leaving.
   Won't You take him when he comes to Your door?
   Am I in heaven here or am I in hell?
   At the crossroads I am standing.

I Love You

Words and Music by Sarah McLachlan

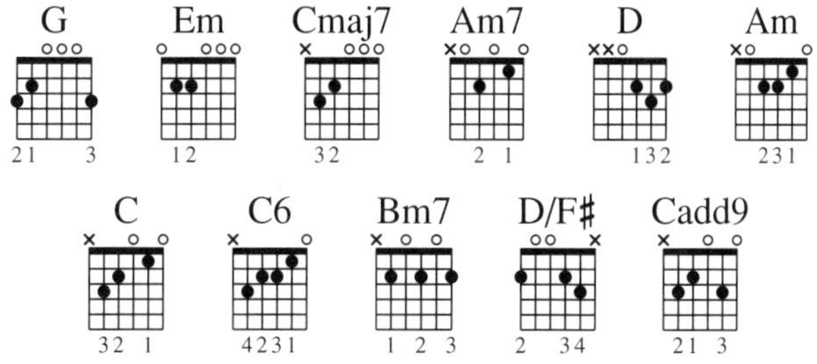

Strum Pattern: 1, 3
Pick Pattern: 2, 4

Am G D
tween us could be miles. Let me sur-round you, my
Em C D
sea to your shore. Let me be the calm you seek.
Pre-Chorus
Am7 D
Oh, and ev - 'ry time I'm close to you, there's too much I can't
Am C D C6 Bm7
say, and you just walk a - way. And
Chorus
G D/F# Em Cmaj7 C6
I for - got to tell you I

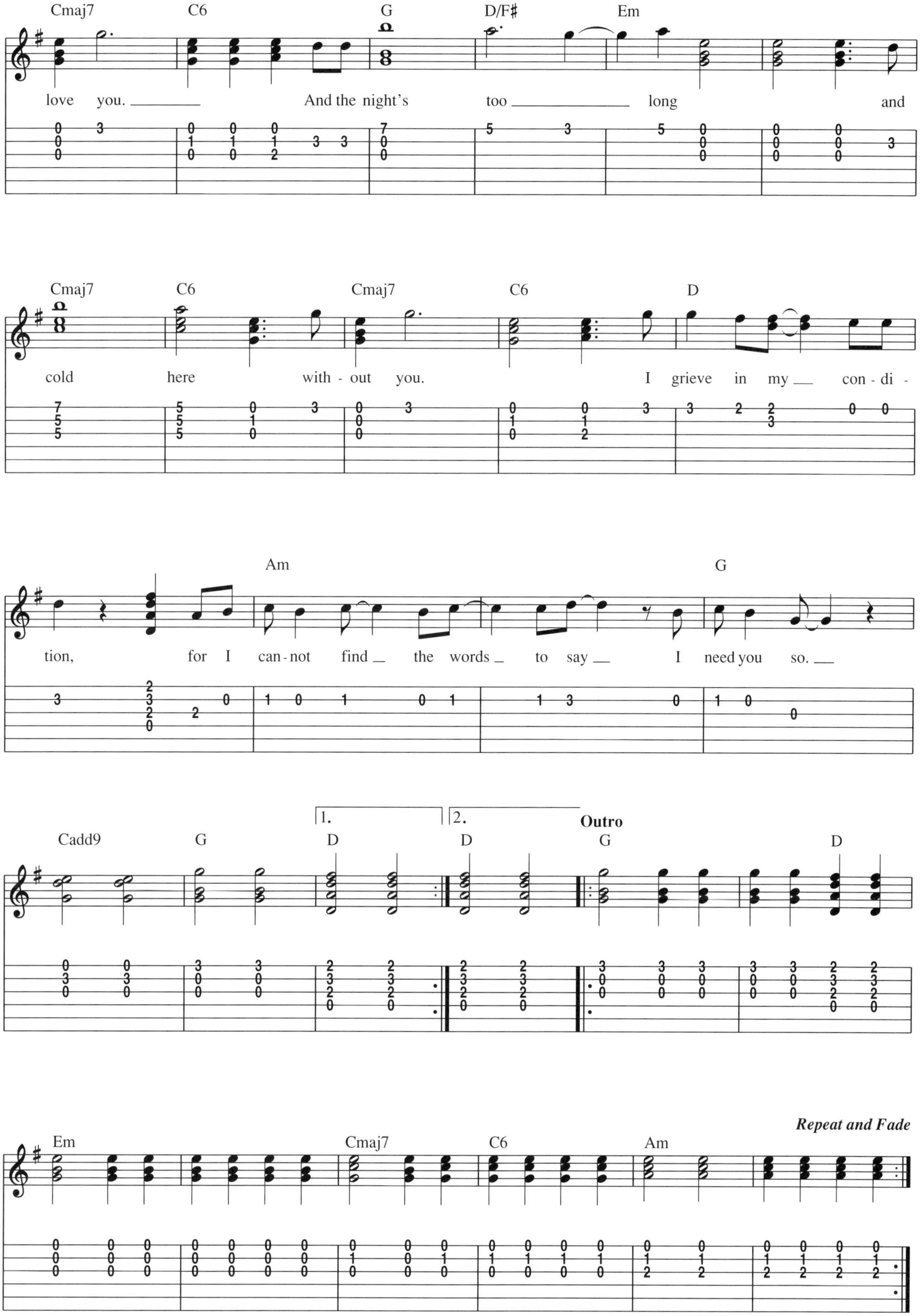
Cmaj7 C6 G D/F♯ Em
love you. And the night's too long and
Cmaj7 C6 Cmaj7 C6 D
cold here with - out you. I grieve in my con - di -
Am G
tion, for I can - not find the words to say I need you so.
1. 2.
Outro
Cadd9 G D D G D
Repeat and Fade
Em Cmaj7 C6 Am

Ice

Words and Music by Sarah McLachlan

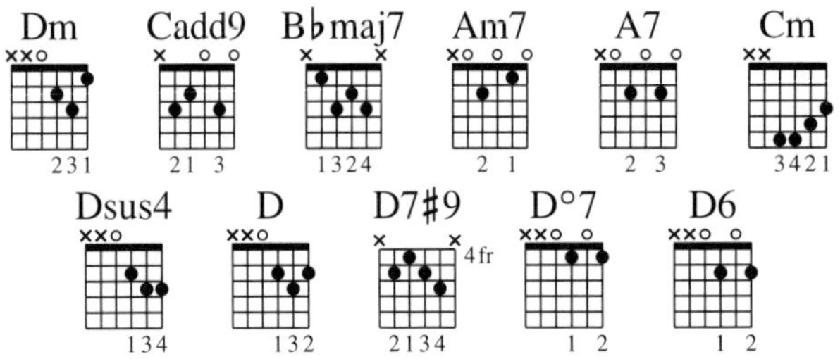

Strum Pattern: 1, 2
Pick Pattern: 2, 4

Additional Lyrics

2. I think you worried for me then;
   The subtle ways that I'd give in,
   But I know you liked the show.
   Tied down to this bed of shame,
   You tried to move around the pain.
   But oh, your soul is anchored.

3. Well, I don't like your tragic sighs
   As if your god has passed you by.
   Well, hey fool, that's your deception.
   Your angels speak with jilted tongues.
   The serpent's tale has come undone.
   You have not strength to squander.

Ice Cream

Words and Music by Sarah McLachlan

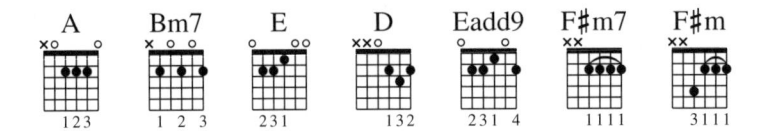

Strum Pattern: 7, 8
Pick Pattern: 7, 8

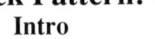

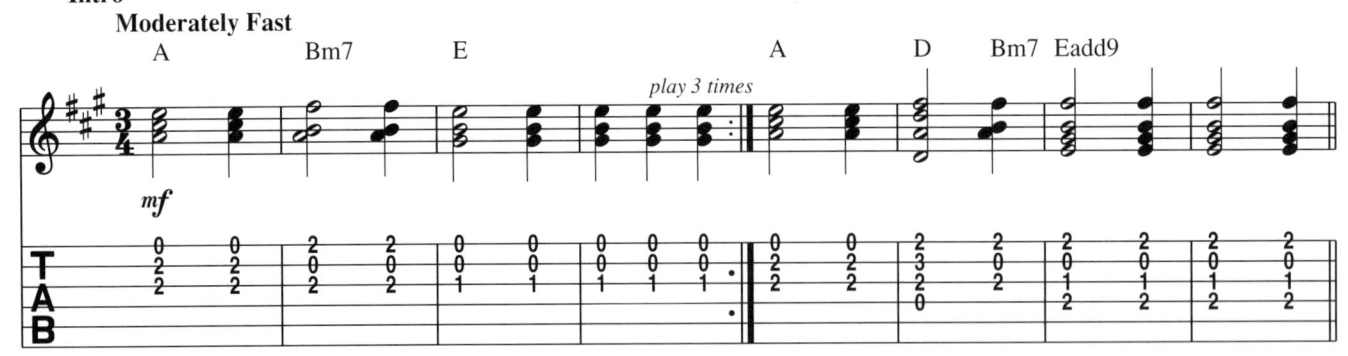

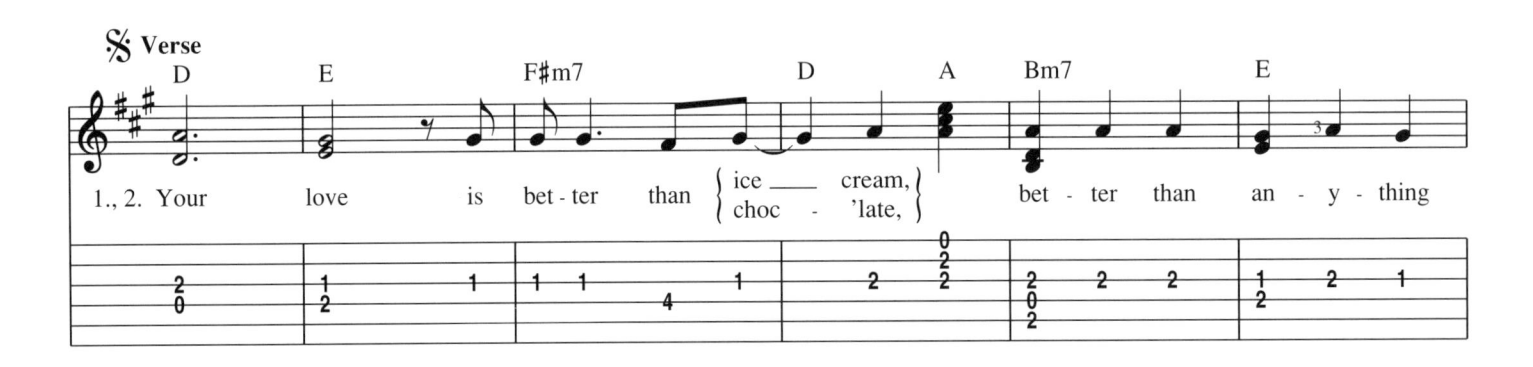

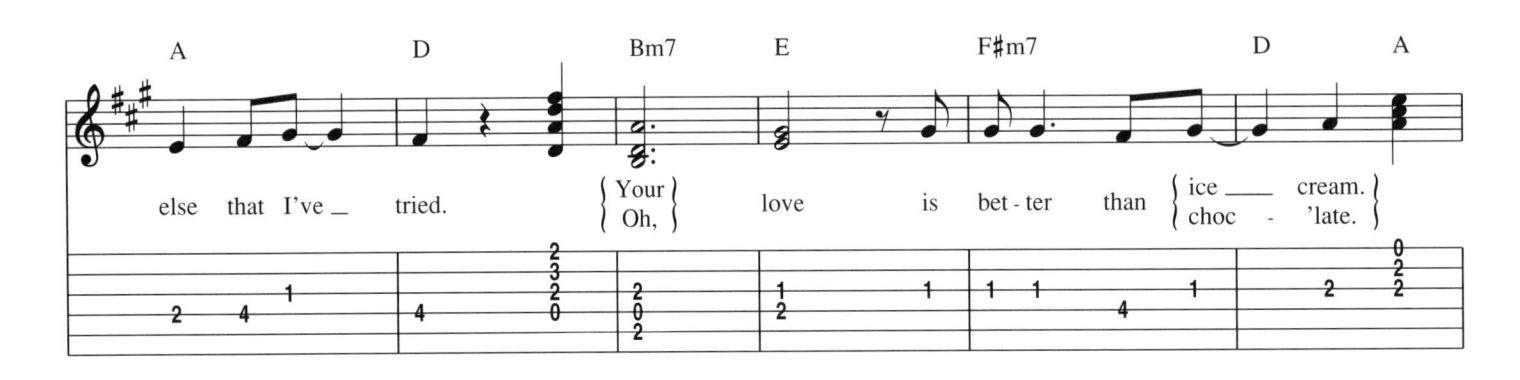

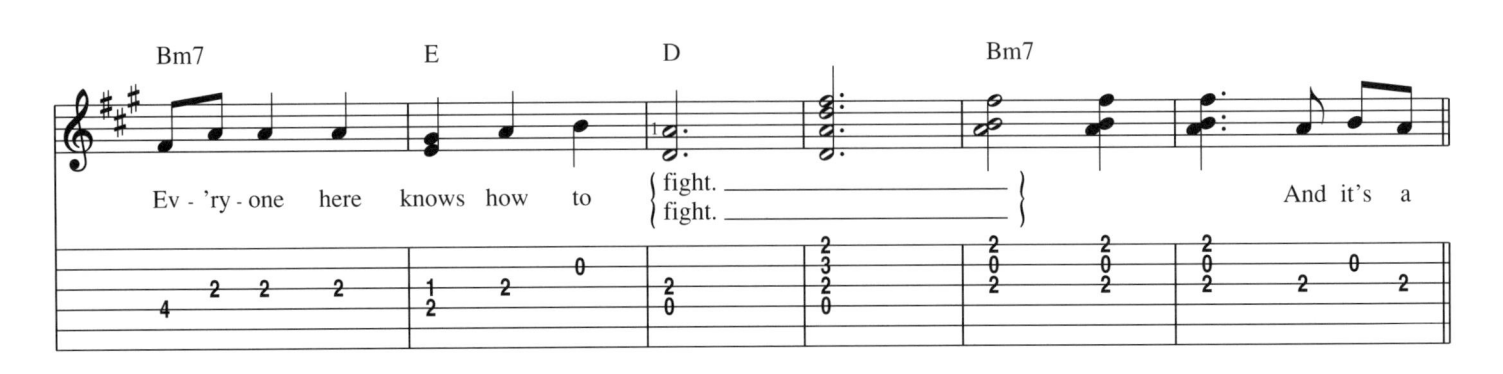

Chorus
F♯m E Bm7 F♯m E
long way down. It's a long way
Bm7 F♯m E Bm7 D A
down. It's a long way down to the place where we
To Coda
Interlude
D A F♯m A Bm7
start - ed from.
2nd time, D.S. al Coda
Coda
E A D A
Do, do, do, do, do, do, do.
Outro
Repeat and Fade
F♯m A Bm7 E
Do, do, do, do, do, do, do.

Mary

Words and Music by Sarah McLachlan

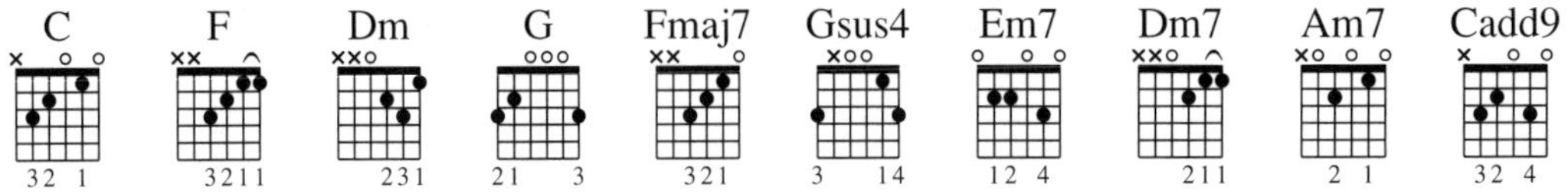

Strum Pattern: 6
Pick Pattern: 4

Intro
Moderately

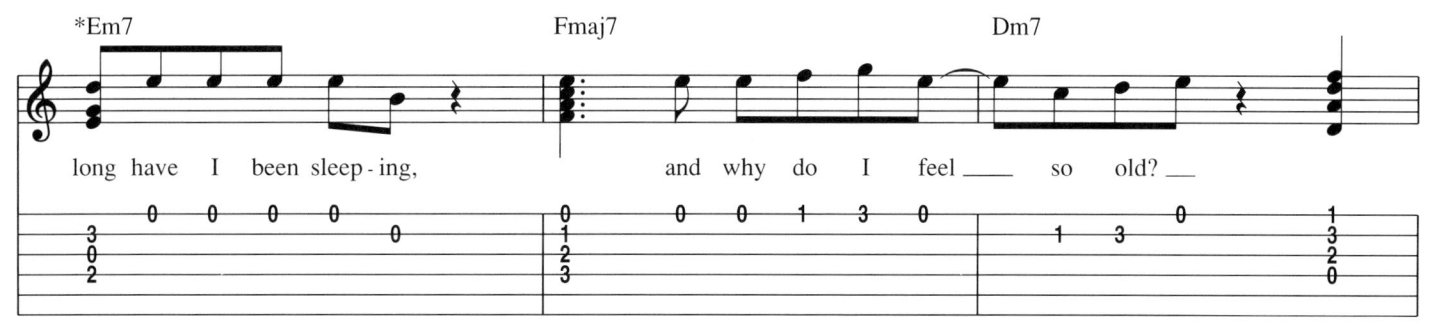

*Use Cadd9, 2nd time.

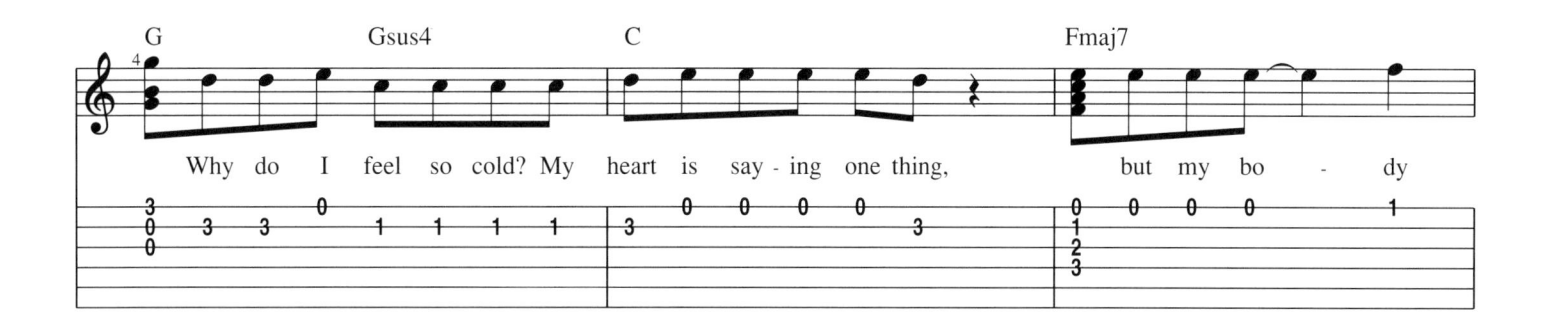

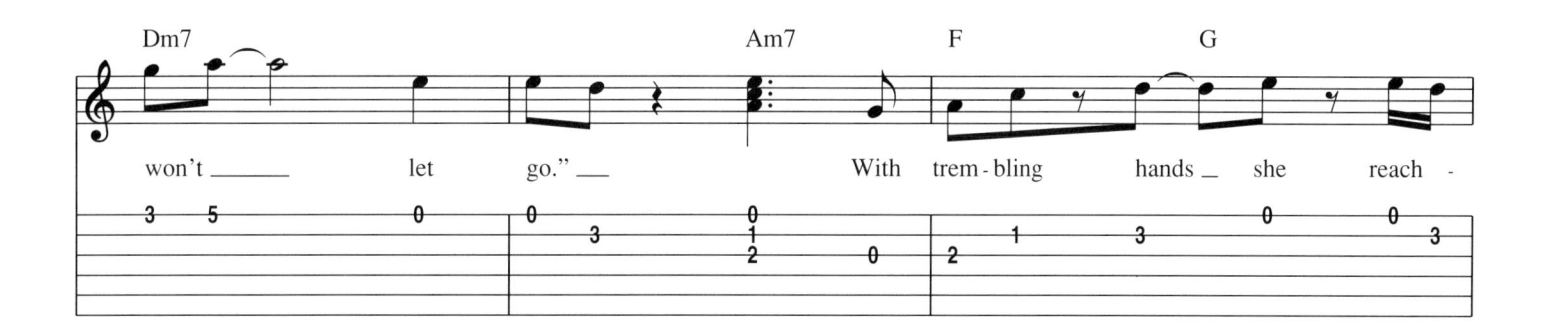

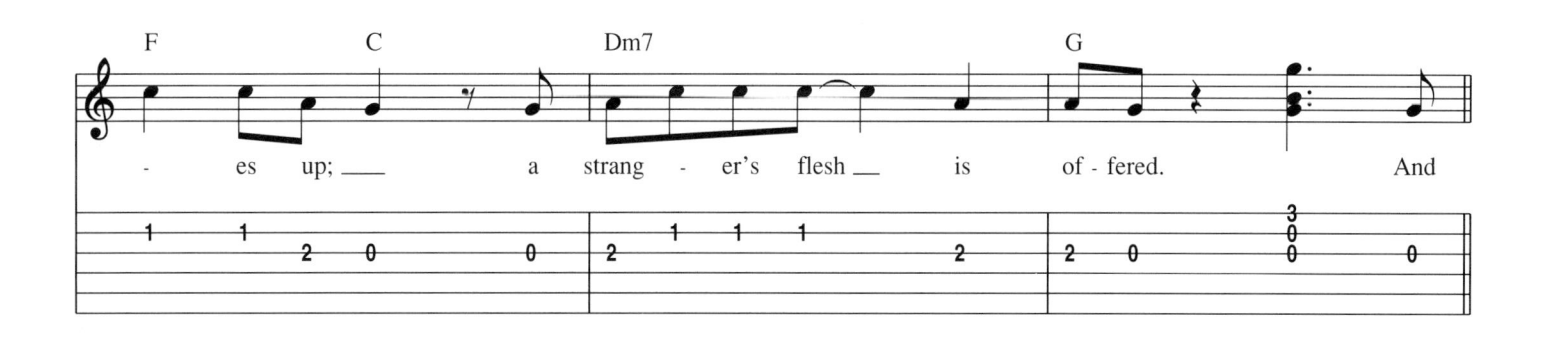

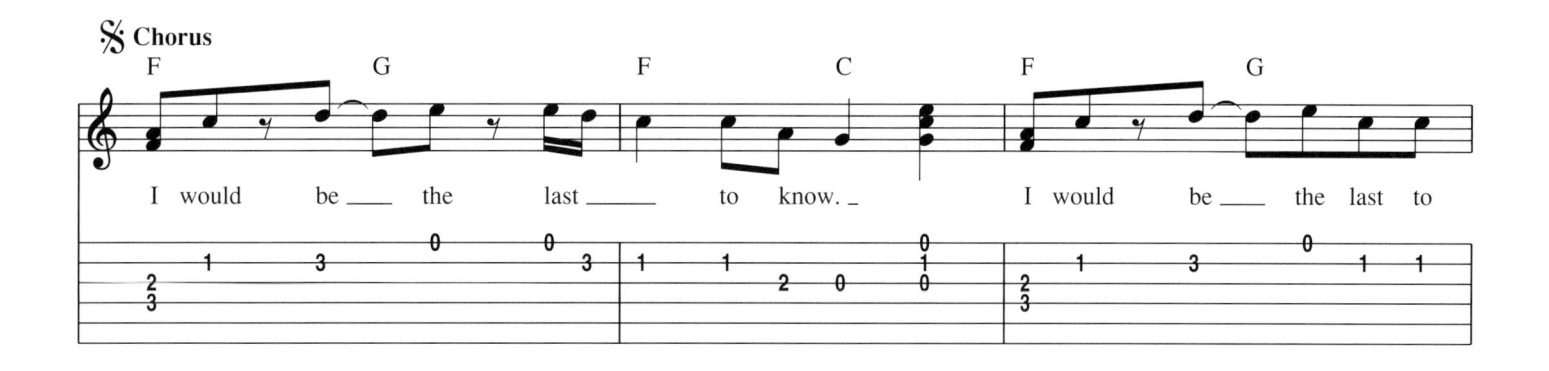

long have I been sleep-ing, and why do I feel so old? Why do I feel so cold? My heart is say-ing one thing, but my bo-dy won't let go." With trem-bling hands she reach-es up; a strang-er's flesh is of-fered. And

Chorus

I would be the last to know. I would be the last to

Additional Lyrics

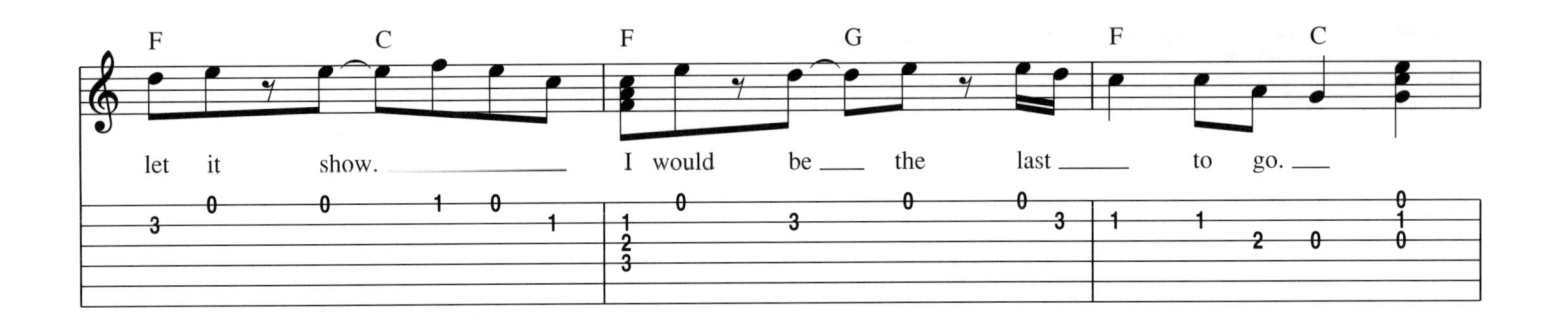

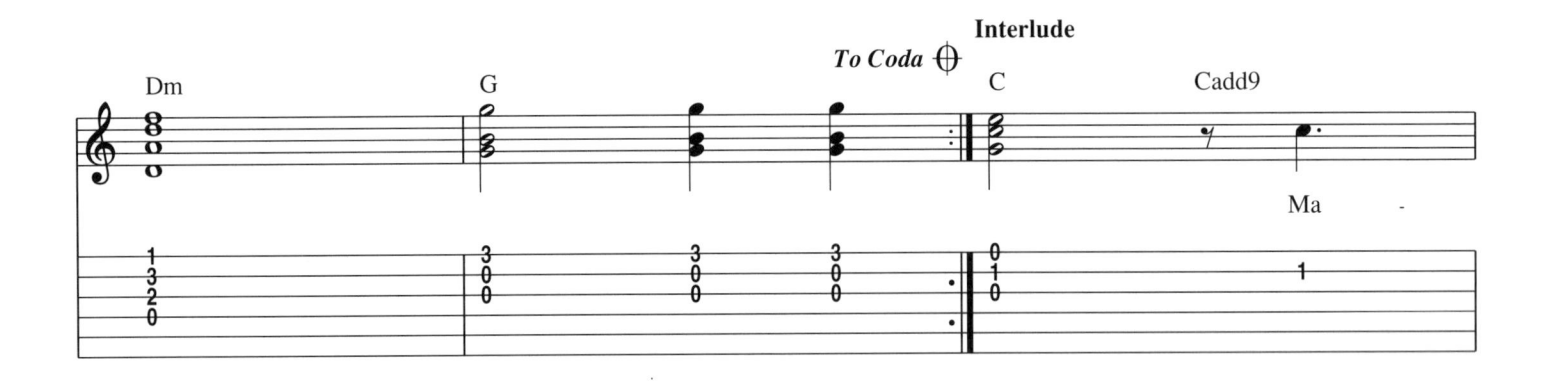

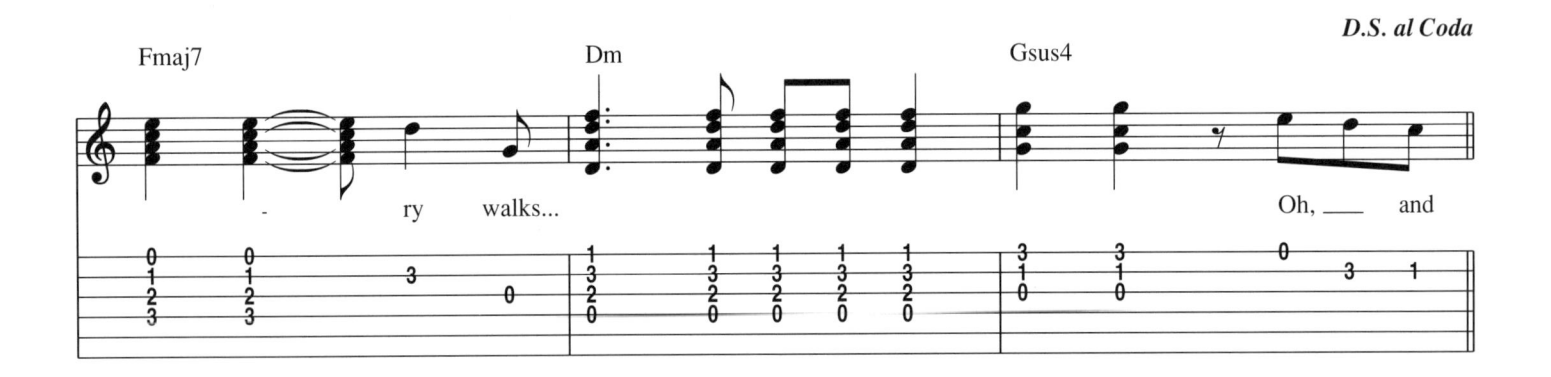

2. Take her hand; she will lead you through the fire,
   Oh, and give you back hope and hope that you don't take too much.
   Respecting what is left, she cradled us.
   Oh, she held us in her arms.
   Unselfish in her suff'ring, she could not understand
   That no one seemed to have the time to cherish what was given.
   Oh, and...

Plenty

Words and Music by Sarah McLachlan

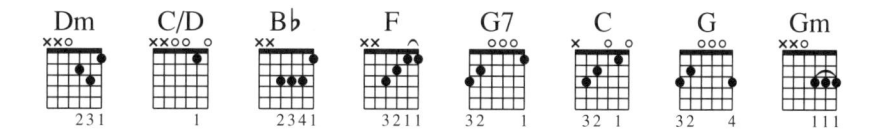

Chords: Dm, C/D, B♭, F, G7, C, G, Gm

Strum Pattern: 2, 6
Pick Pattern: 2, 4

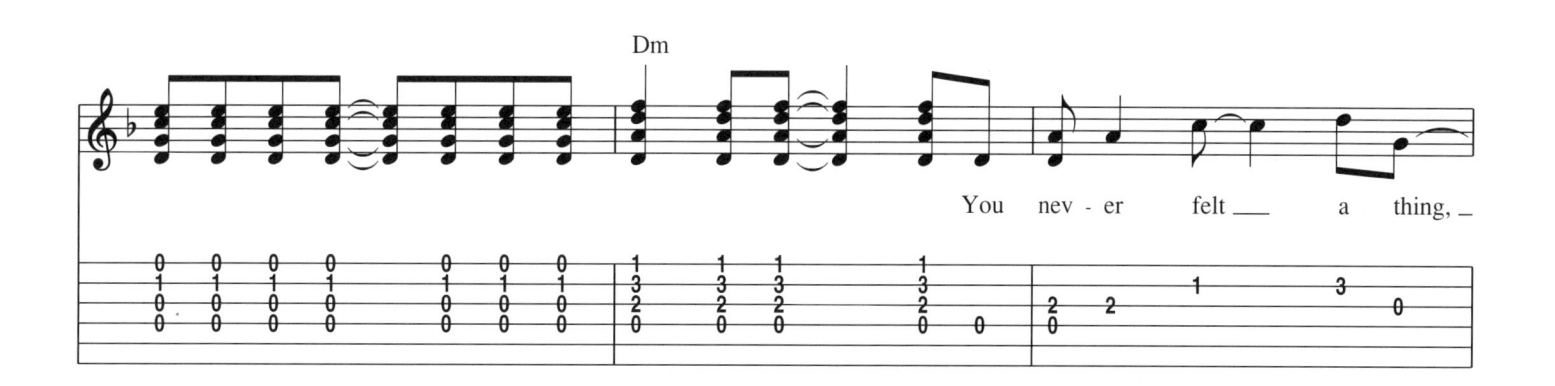

Verse
Moderately

1. I looked in - to ___ your ___ eyes;
2. *See Additional Lyrics*

they told me plen - ty I al - read - y knew.

You nev - er felt ___ a thing, ___

Copyright © 1993 Sony/ATV Songs LLC and Tyde Music
All Rights Administered by Sony/ATV Music Publishing, 8 Music Square West, Nashville, TN 37203
International Copyright Secured   All Rights Reserved

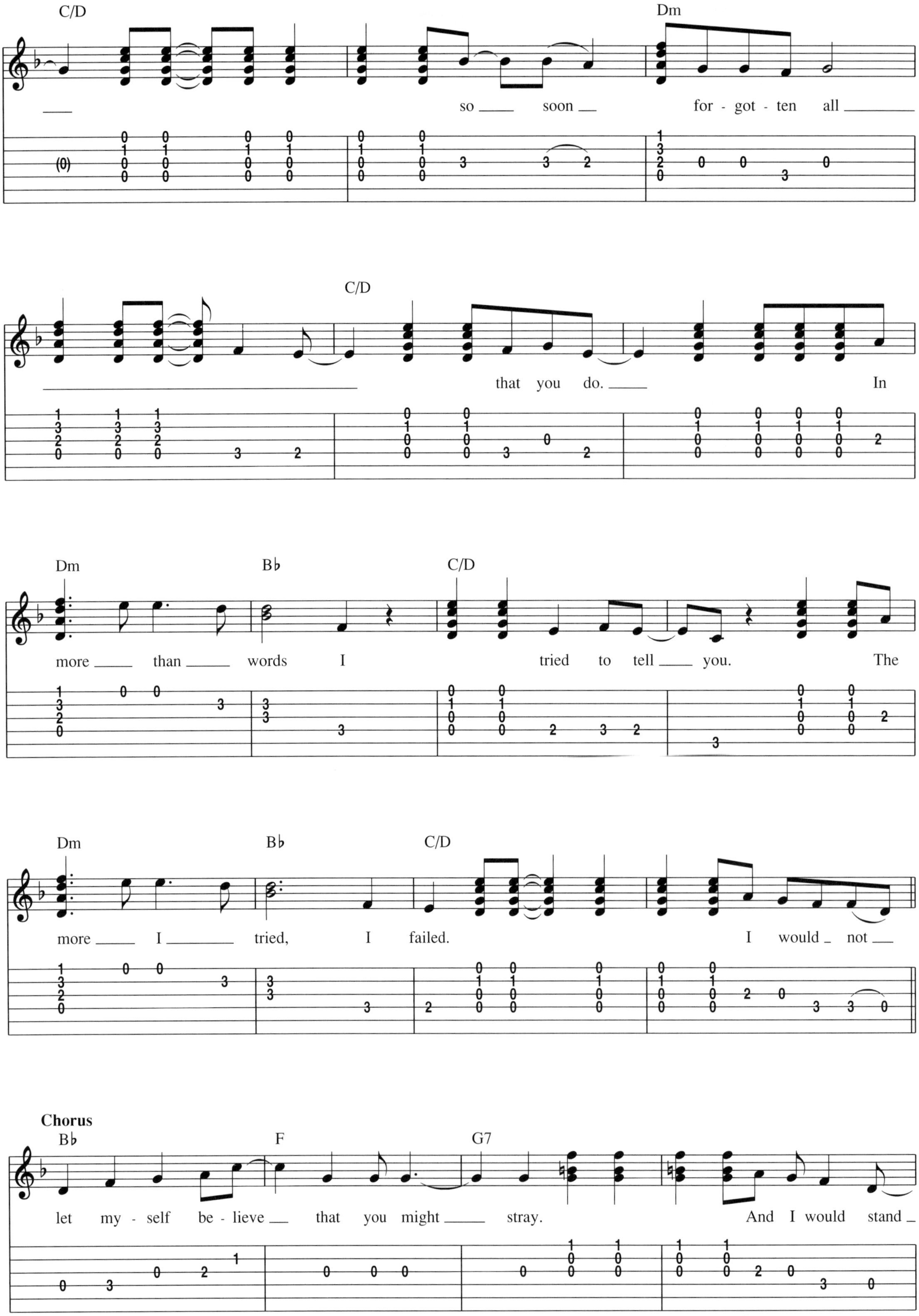
C/D
Dm
so soon for - got - ten all
C/D
that you do. In
Dm
B♭
C/D
more than words I tried to tell you. The
Dm
B♭
C/D
more I tried, I failed. I would not
Chorus
B♭
F
G7
let my - self be - lieve that you might stray. And I would stand

Additional Lyrics

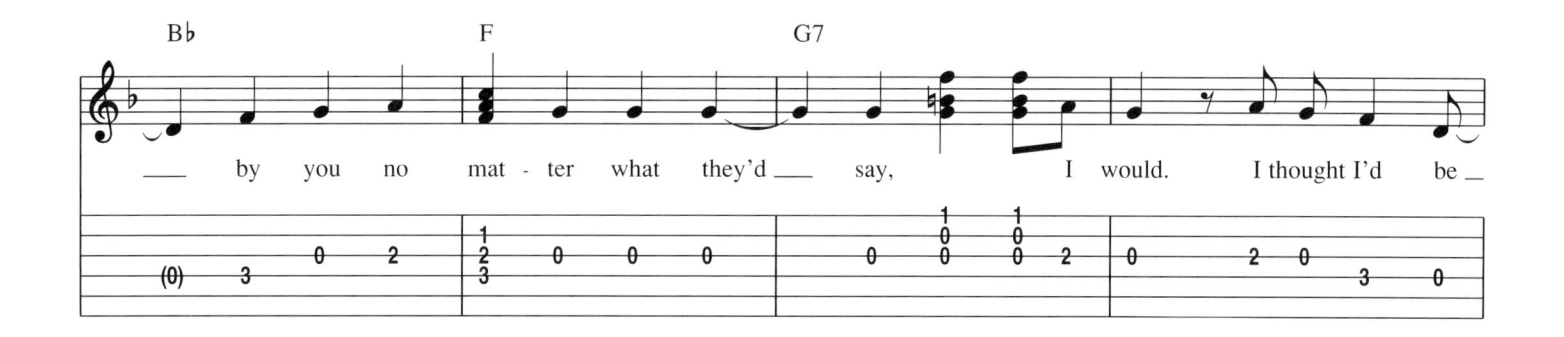

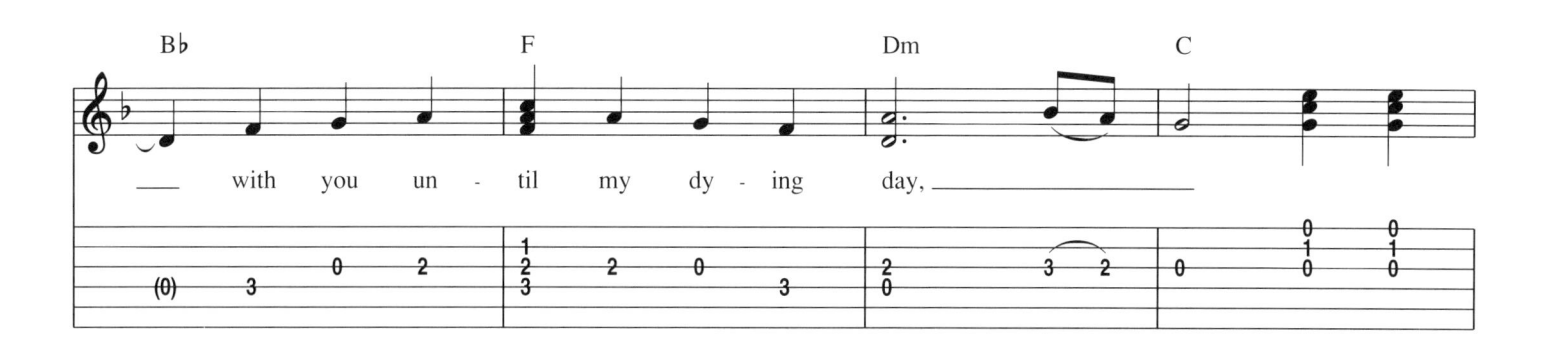

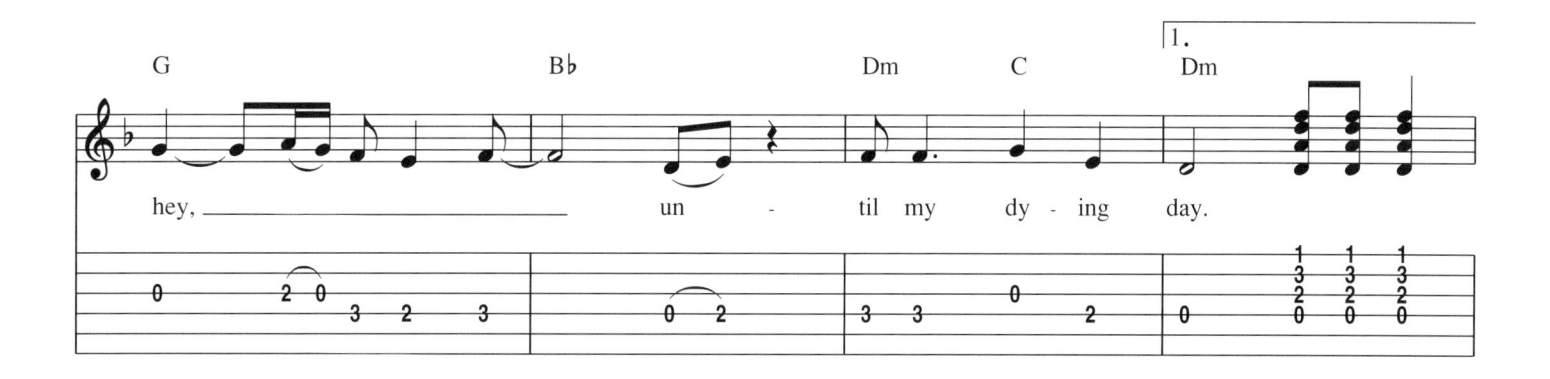

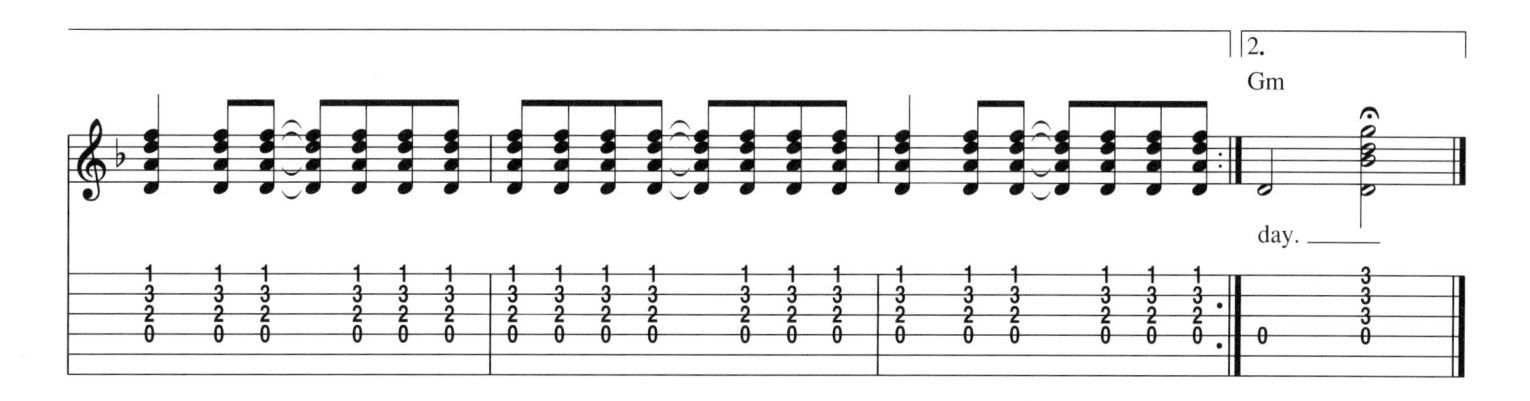

2. I used to think my life was often empty,
   A lonely space to fill.
   You hurt me more than I ever could have imagined,
   You made my world stand still.
   And in that stillness there was a freedom
   I never felt before.

Sweet Surrender

Words and Music by Sarah McLachlan

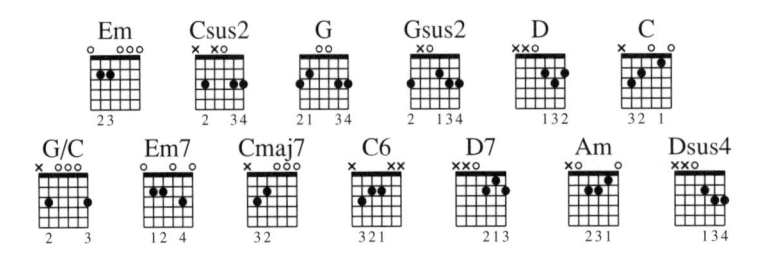

Strum Pattern: 1, 3
Pick Pattern: 3, 4

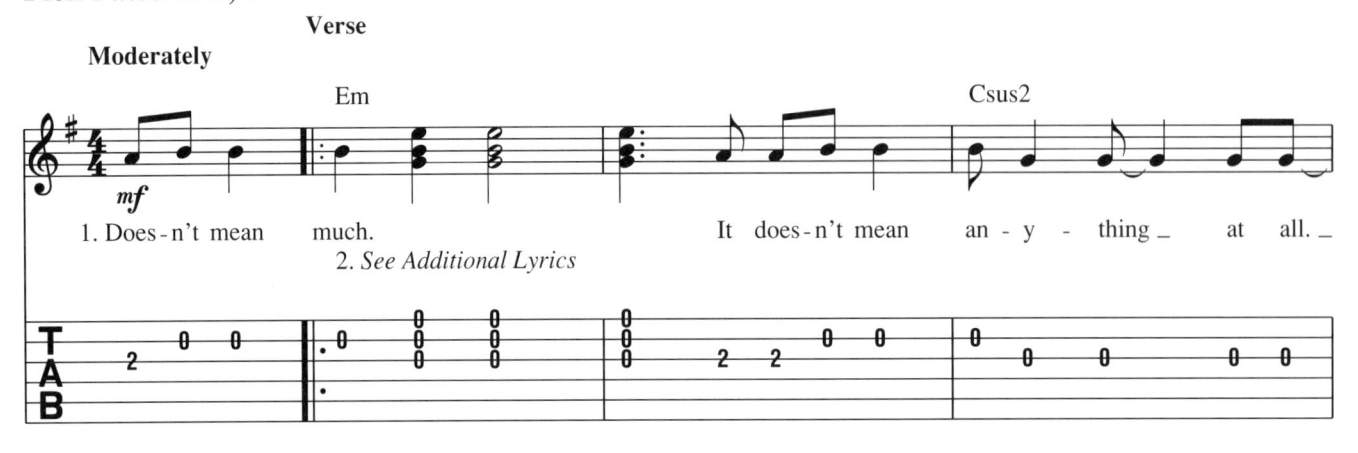

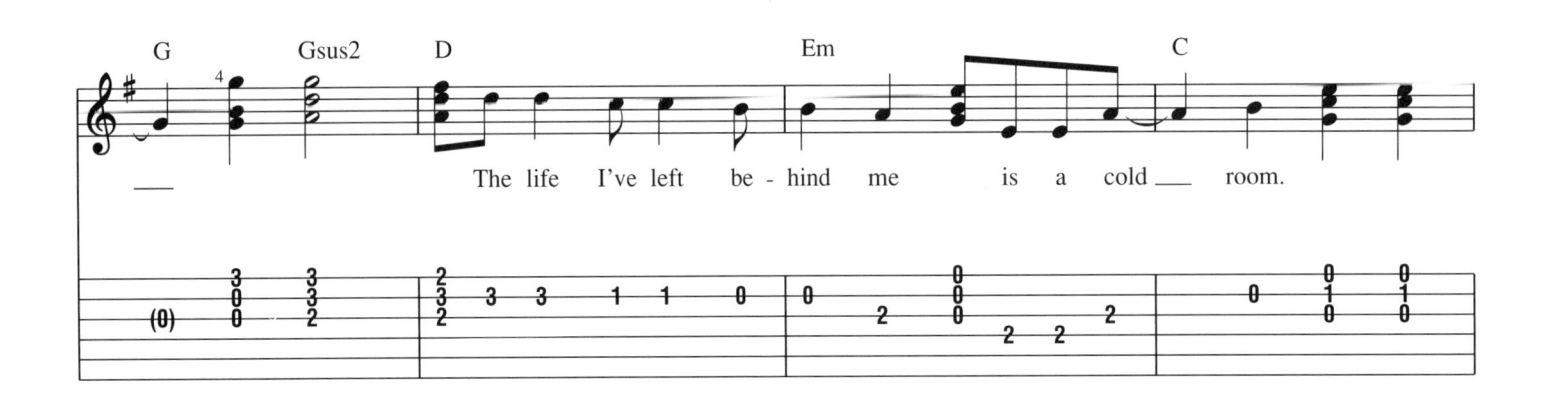

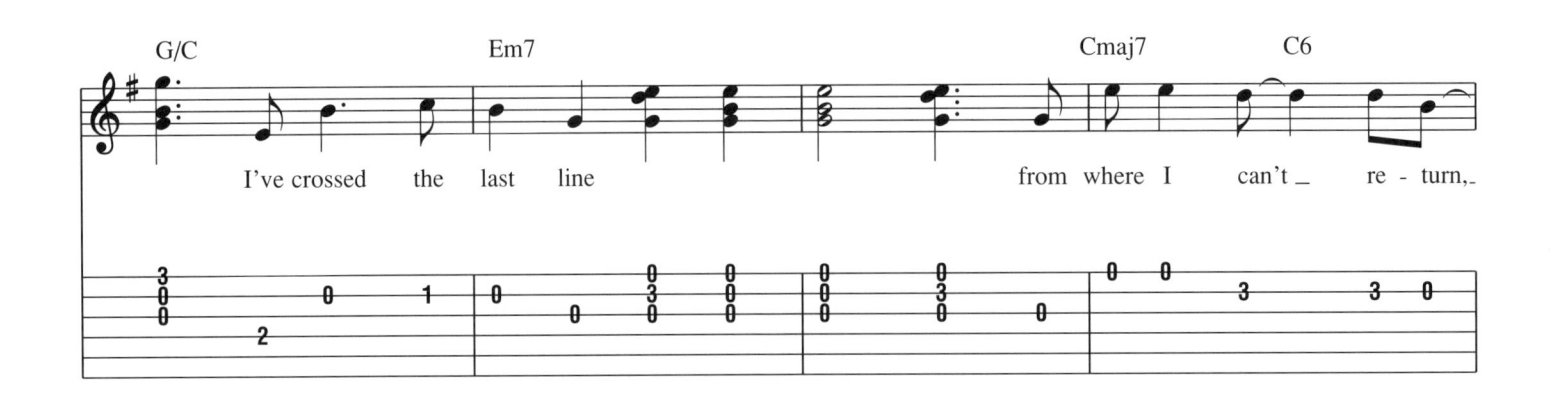

Moderately — *Verse*

1. Does-n't mean much. It does-n't mean an-y-thing at all.
2. *See Additional Lyrics*

The life I've left be-hind me is a cold room.

I've crossed the last line from where I can't re-turn,

Copyright © 1997 Sony/ATV Songs LLC and Tyde Music
All Rights Administered by Sony/ATV Music Publishing, 8 Music Square West, Nashville, TN 37203
International Copyright Secured All Rights Reserved

G Gsus2 D Em7 Cmaj7 C6
where ev - 'ry step I took in faith be - trayed me.
G Gsus2 D Em7 Cmaj7 C6 Cmaj7 C6
And led me from my home.
Chorus
D Csus2 G Em7
Sweet sur - ren - der
C D7 G Gsus2 G Gsus2
1.
is all that I have to give. 2. Take me
2.
Em7 D Csus2
to give. Sweet

To Coda
G Em7 C D7
surren-der is all that I have
G Bridge Am
to give. And I don't un-der-stand how the
D G
touch of your hand I would be
C
the one to fall. I miss the
Am Dsus4 D
lit-tle things. I miss

Additional Lyrics

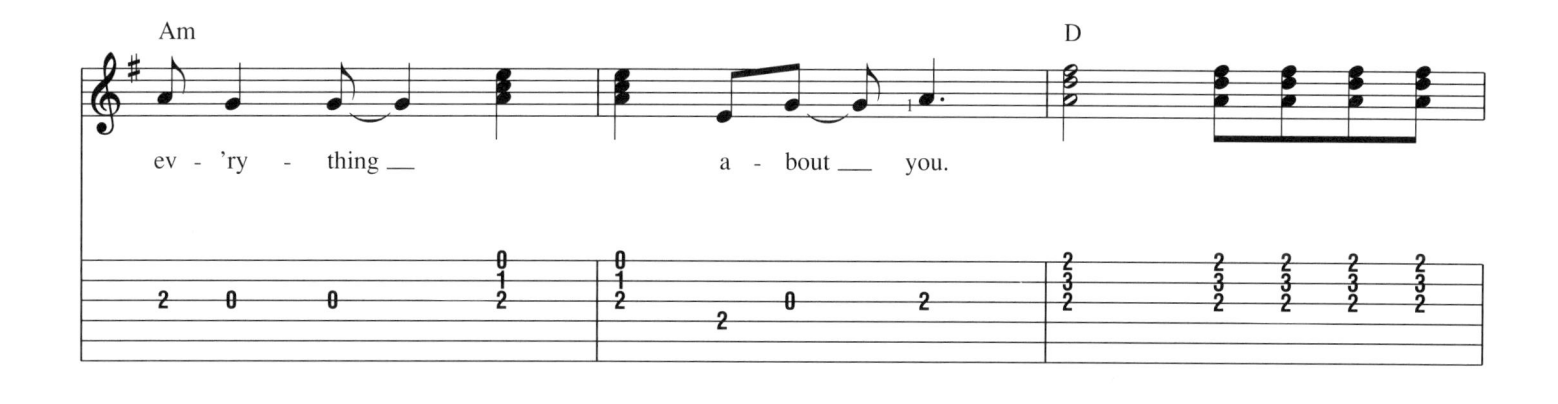

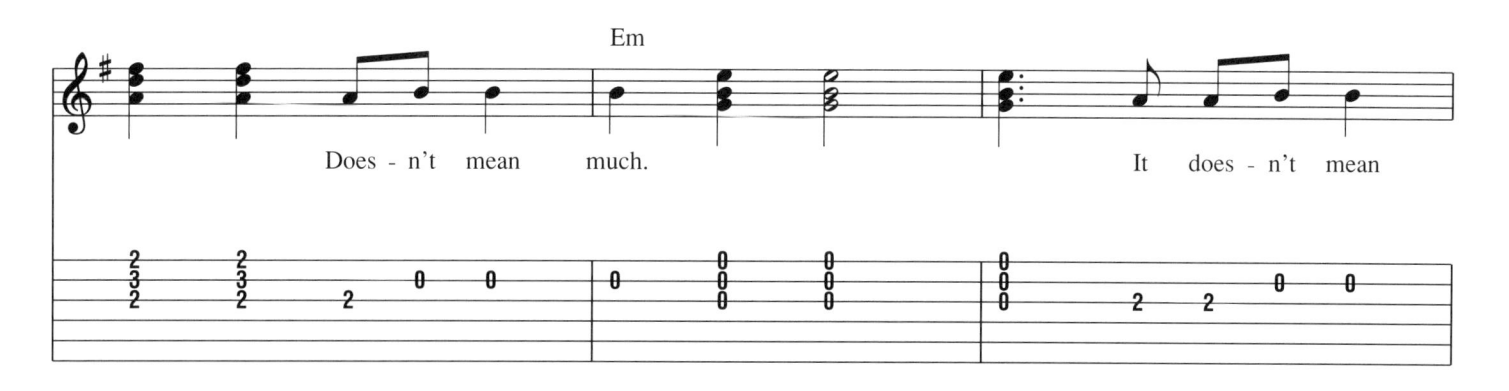

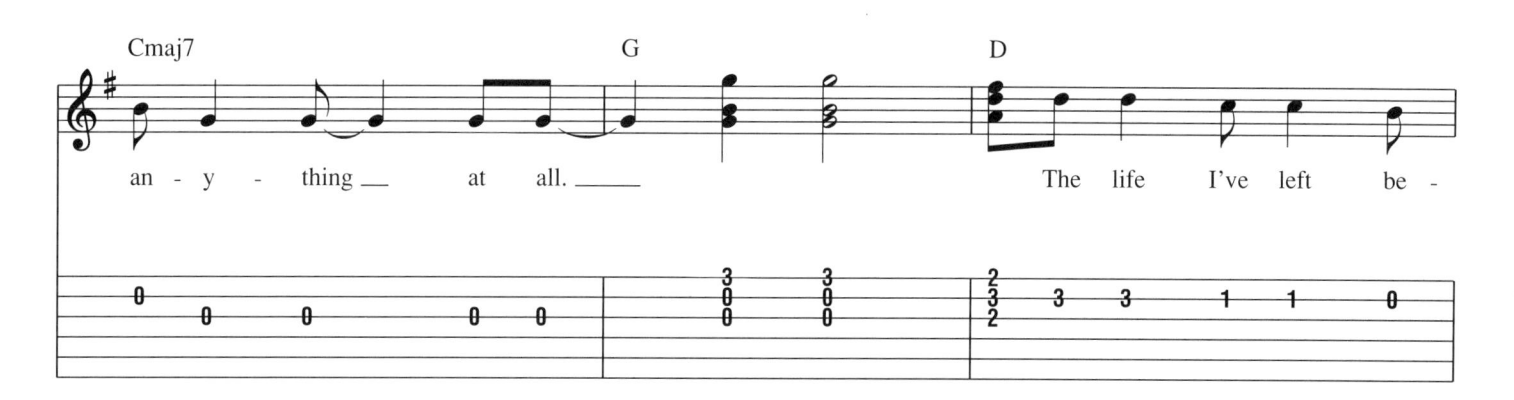

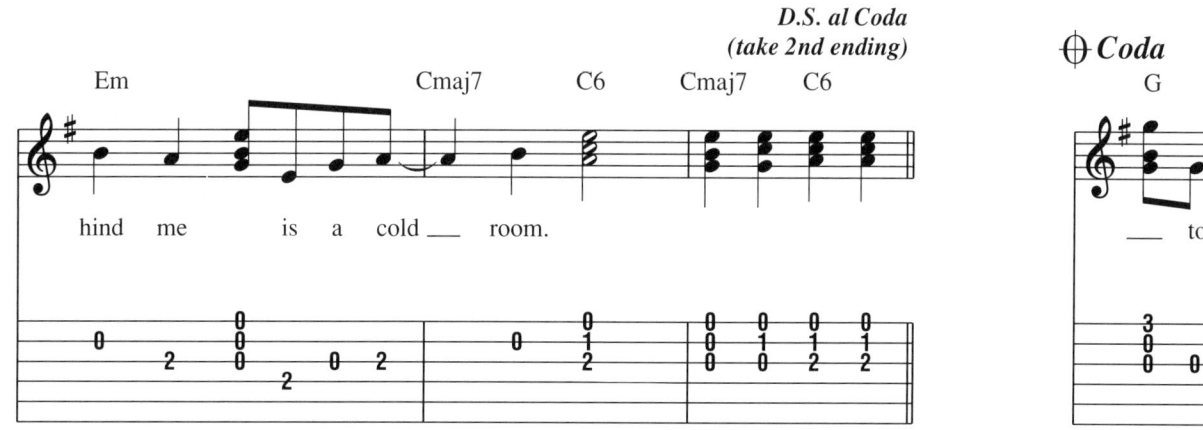

2. Take me in, no questions asked.
   You strip away the ugliness that surrounds me.
   Are you an angel?
   Am I already that gone?
   I only hope that I won't disappoint you.
   When I'm down here on my knees…

Possession

Words and Music by Sarah McLachlan

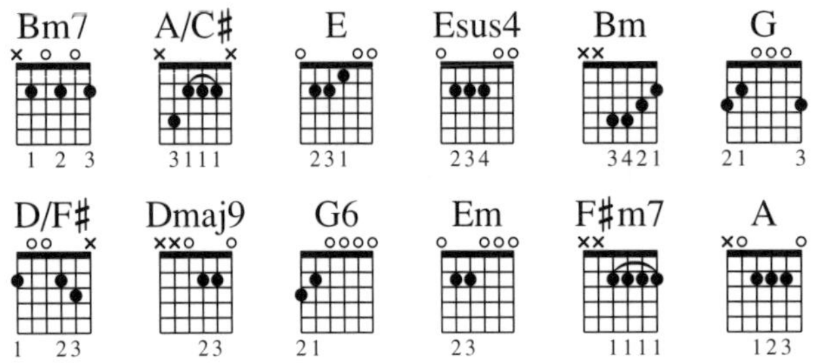

Strum Pattern: 2, 6
Pick Pattern: 4, 6

E Esus4 G Bm
guide. Would I spend for - ev - er here and
Esus4 E G D/F♯
not be sat - is - fied? And I would be the one
Chorus
Bm Dmaj9 G G6 D/F♯
to hold you down, kiss you so hard. I'll take your breath a -
To Coda
G Bm Dmaj9 Em F♯m7
way. And af - ter I'd wipe a - way the tears. Just close your eyes,
1. Bm A/C♯
dear.
2. Bm
dear.

Additional Lyrics

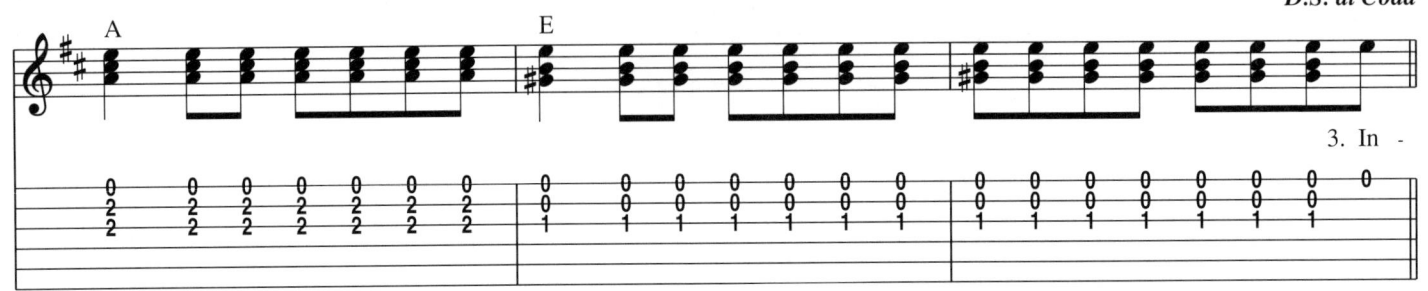

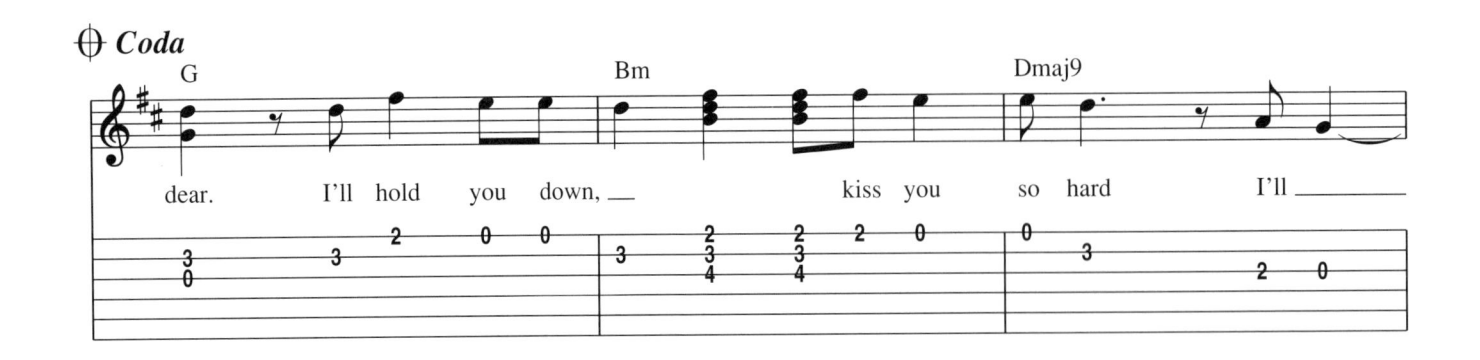

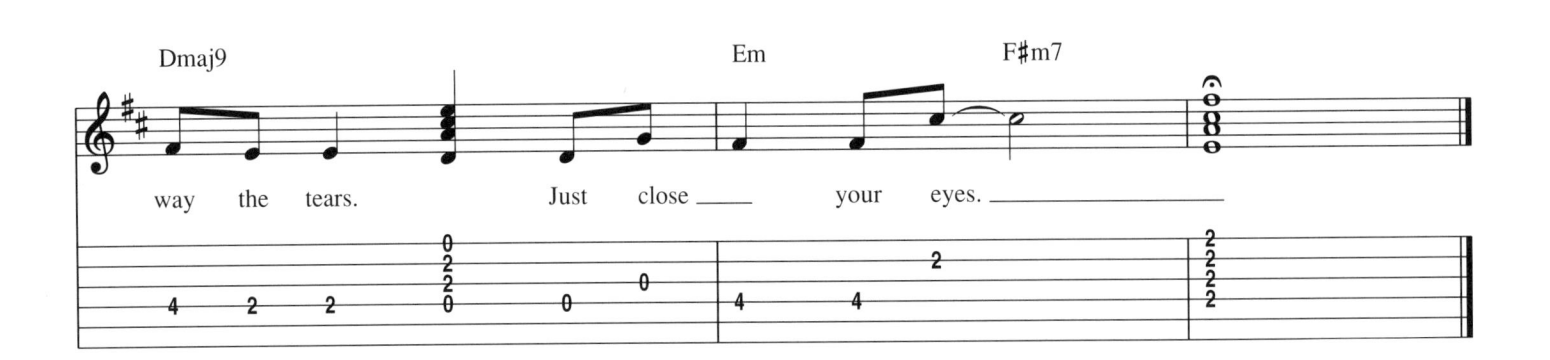

2. Through this world I've stumbled,
   So many times betrayed,
   Tryin' to find an honest word
   To find the truth enslaved.
   Oh, you speak to me in riddles
   And you speak to me in rhyme.
   My body aches to breathe your breath,
   Your words keep me alive.

3. Into this night I wander,
   It's morning that I dread.
   Another day of knowing of
   The path I fear to tread.
   Oh, into the sea of waking dreams
   I follow without pride,
   'Cause nothing stands between us here
   And I won't be denied.

Wait

Words and Music by Sarah McLachlan

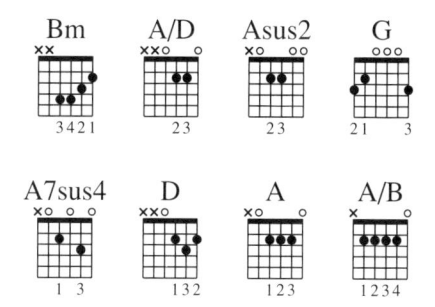

Bm A/D Asus2 G

A7sus4 D A A/B

Strum Pattern: 1, 6
Pick Pattern: 2, 4

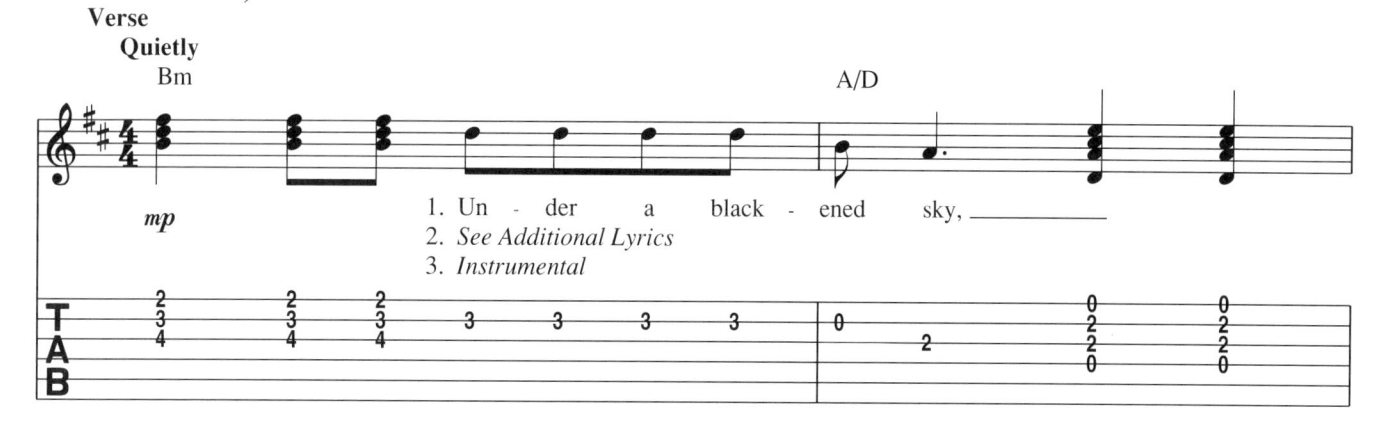

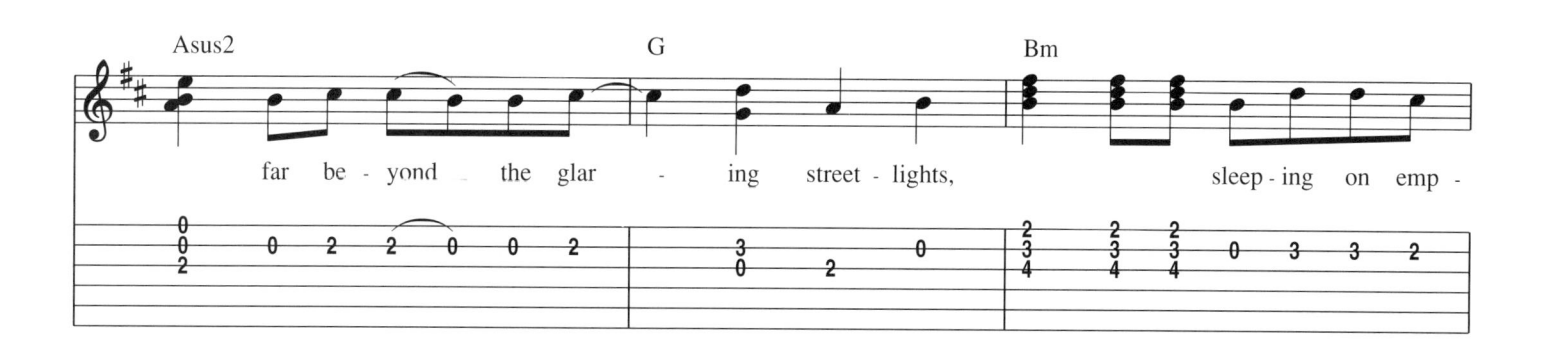

Verse
Quietly

1. Under a blackened sky,
2. *See Additional Lyrics*
3. *Instrumental*

far beyond the glaring streetlights, sleeping on empty dreams, the vultures lie in wait.

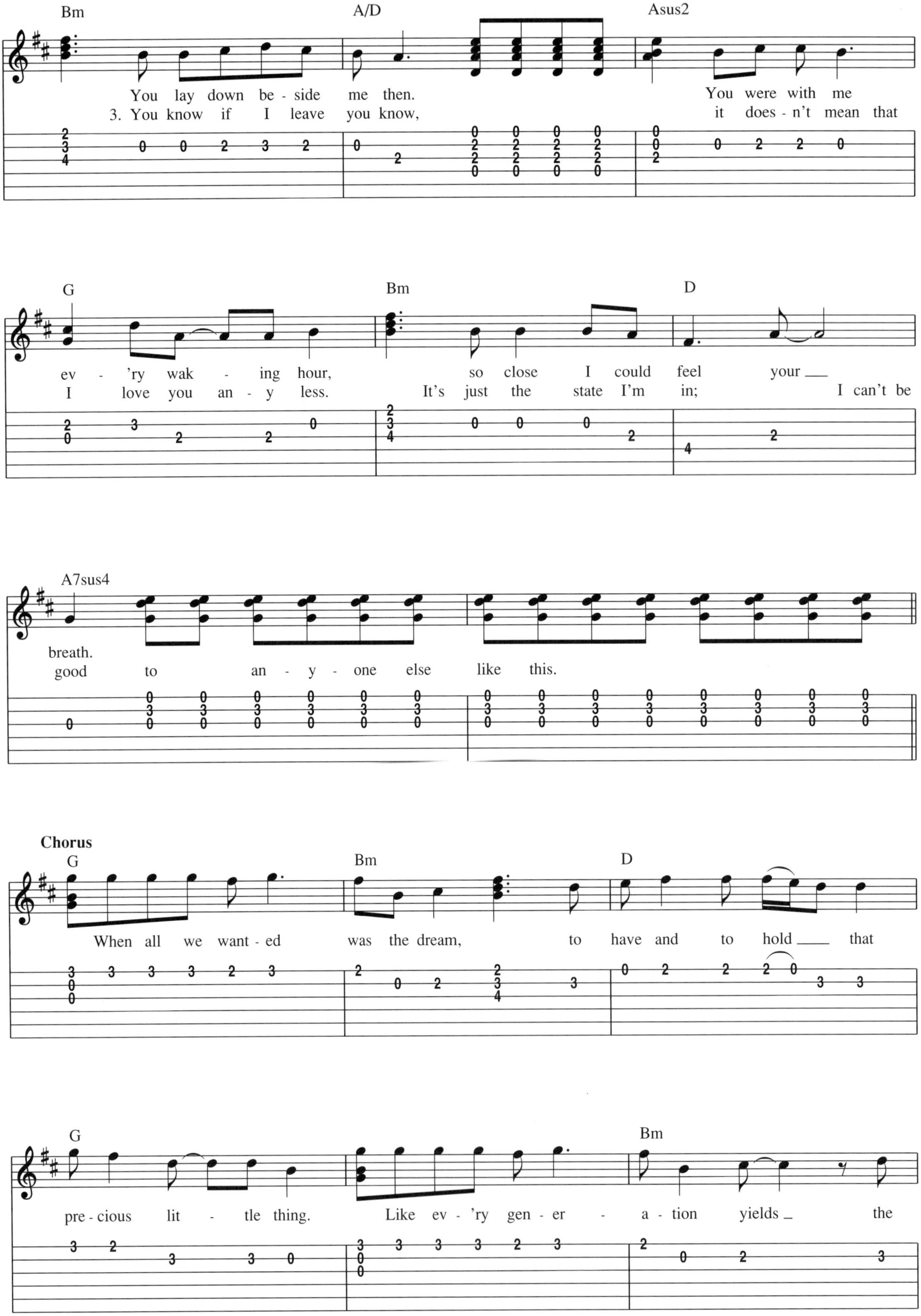
Bm
A/D
Asus2
You lay down be - side me then. You were with me
3. You know if I leave you know, it does - n't mean that
G
Bm
D
ev - 'ry wak - ing hour, so close I could feel your
I love you an - y less. It's just the state I'm in; I can't be
A7sus4
breath.
good to an - y - one else like this.
Chorus
G
Bm
D
When all we want - ed was the dream, to have and to hold that
G
Bm
pre - cious lit - tle thing. Like ev - 'ry gen - er - a - tion yields the

Additional Lyrics

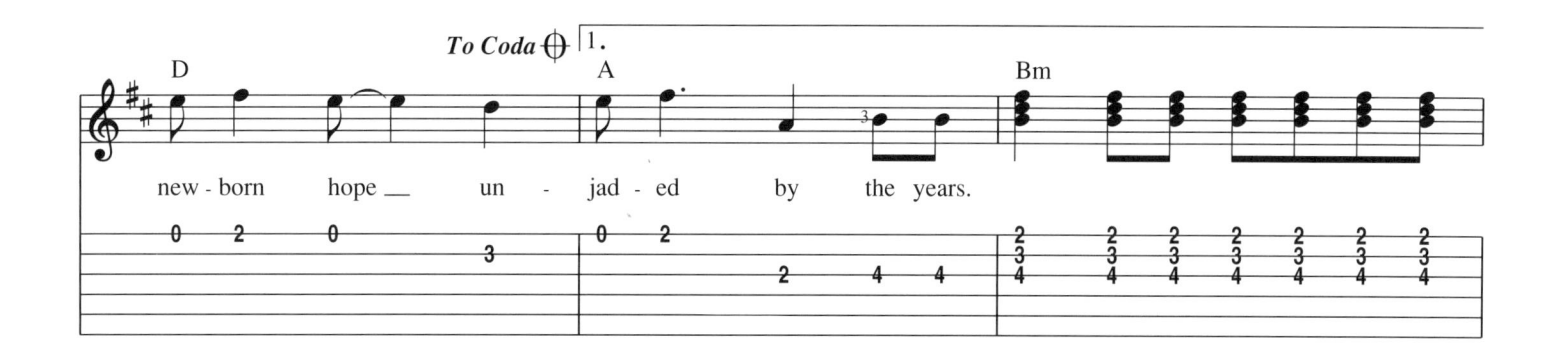

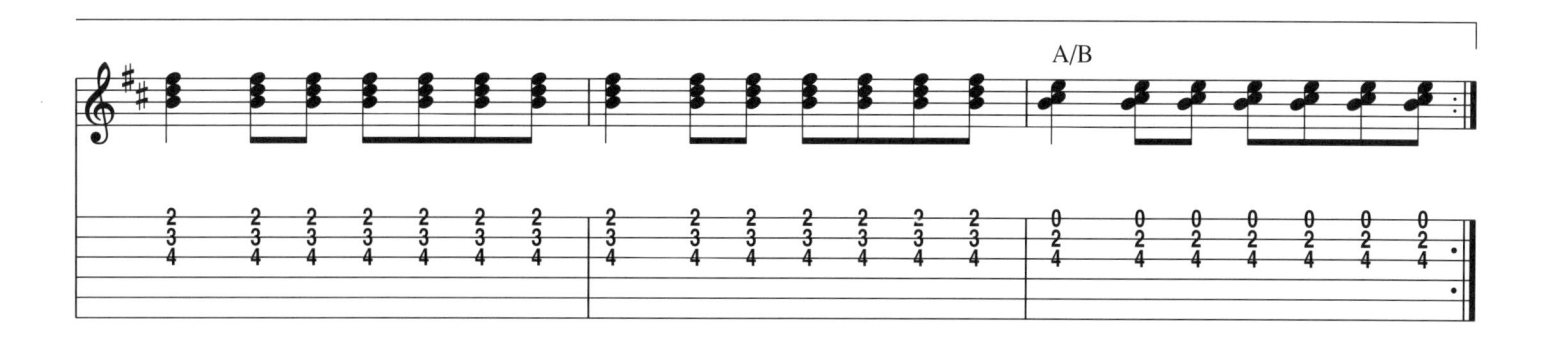

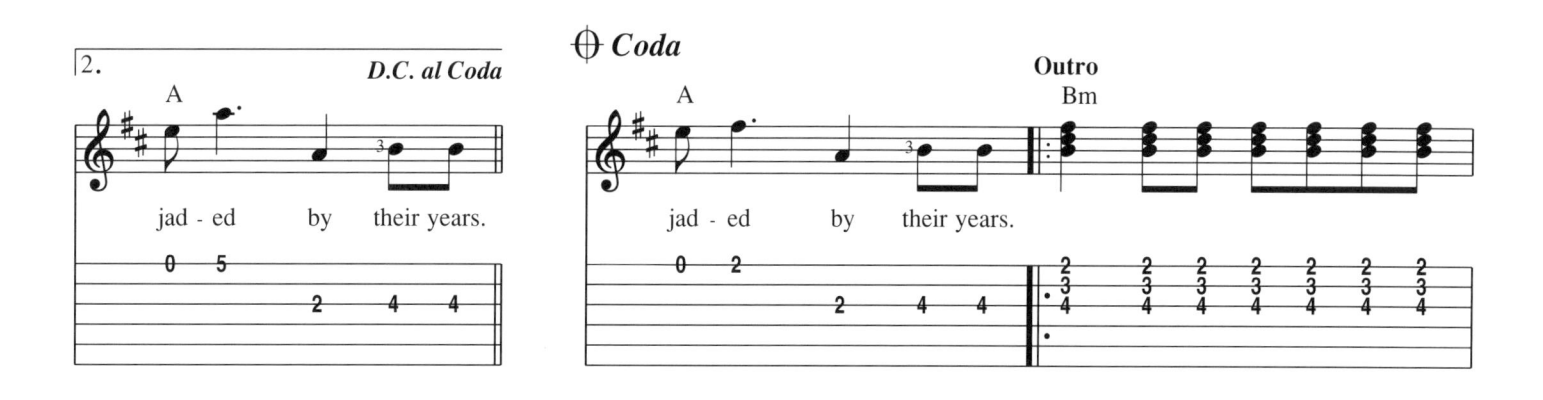

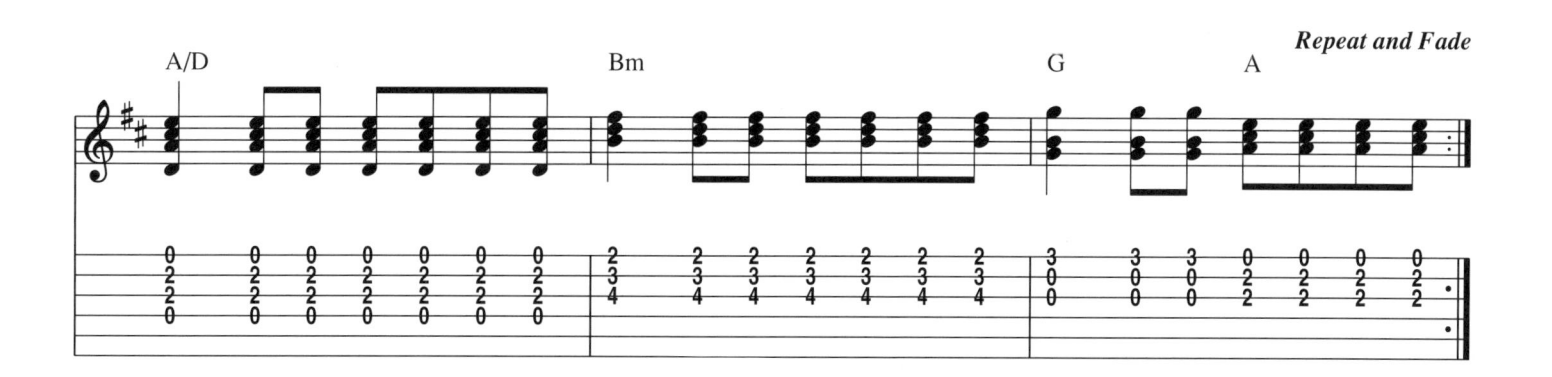

2. Pressed up against the glass,
   I found myself wanting sympathy.
   But to be consumed again,
   Oh, I know would be the death of me.
   There is a love that's inherently given,
   A kind of blindness offered to deceive.
   And in that light of forbidden joy,
   Oh, I know I won't receive it.

Witness

Words and Music by Sarah McLachlan and Pierre Marchand

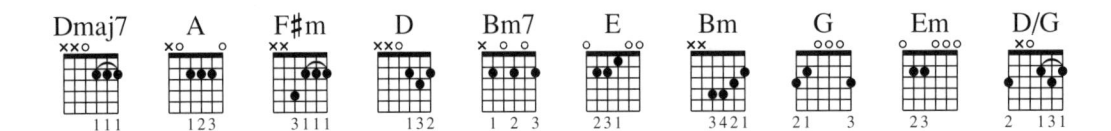

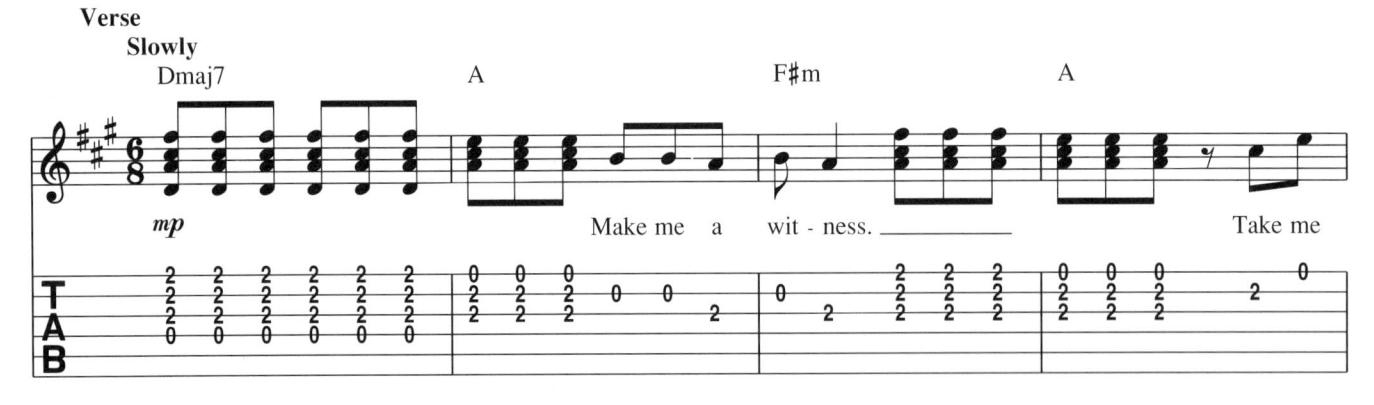

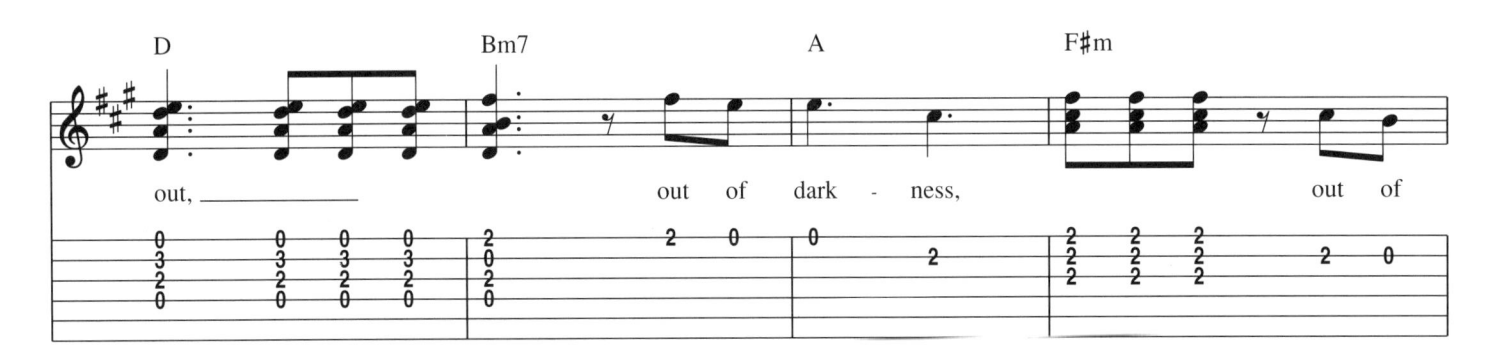

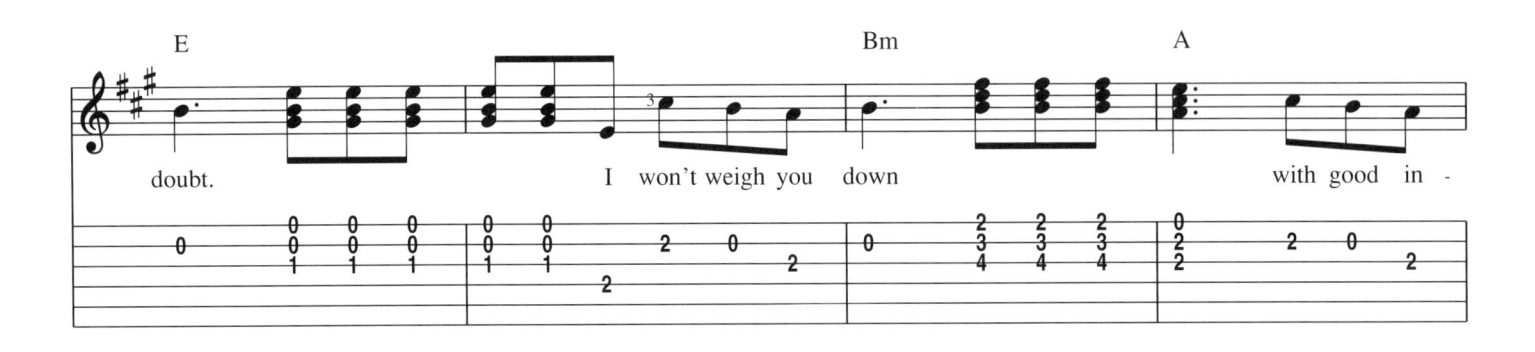

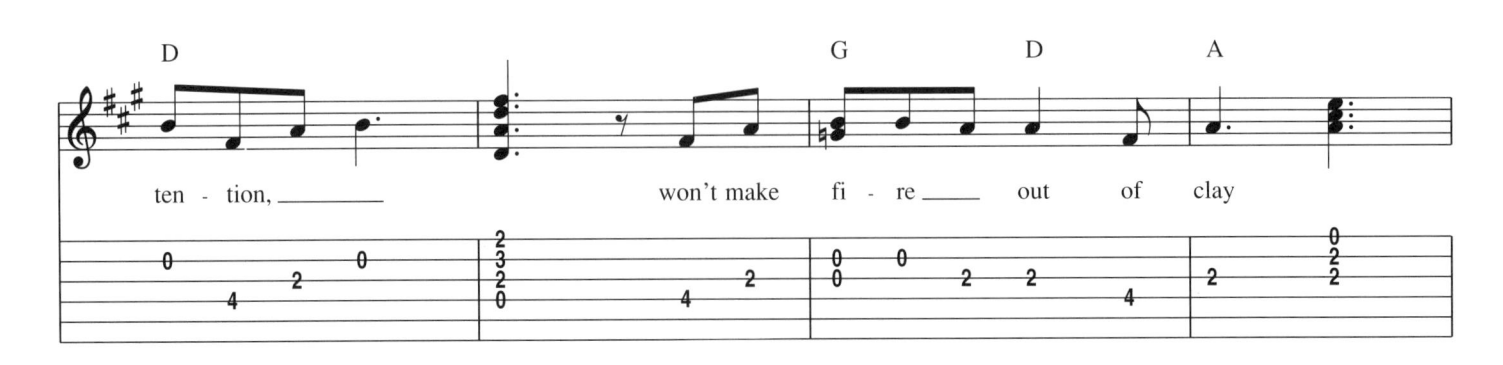

Bm A Em
or oth - er in - ven - tions. Will we
Chorus
D A Em
burn in heav - en like we
D A Em D A
do down here? Will a change come while we're
Em G
4:3
wait-ing? Ev - 'ry-one is wait-ing. And when we're
Bm A D Bm A
done soul - search-ing and we car - ry the weight and die for a

D Bm A D A G
cause, is mis-er-y made beau-ti-ful right be-fore our eyes? Will
D A Bm A Em
mer-cy be re-vealed or blind us where we stand? 1. Will we
Outro
D A Em D A
(3.) burn in heav-en like we do down
2. Instrumental
Em D A Em
here? Will the change come while we're wait-ing? Ev-'ry-one is
4:3
1. 2. 3.
G G D/G N.C. G D/G D
wait-ing. 3. Will we wait-ing.